THE ARK LAW GROUP

COMPLETE GUIDE
to
SHORT SALES

By: Ross Kilburn and Lambros Politis, Esq.

Ark Law Group, PLLC
www.arklawgroup.com
1-800-603-3525

AUROCH PRESS
The Ark Law Group: Complete Guide to Short Sales
Ross Kilburn
Lambros Politis, Esq.

Copyeditor: Jacqueline Windh

Published in the United States by Auroch Press
ISBN-13: 978-0989495318
ISBN-10: 0989495310

Version 2.6
Printed by CreateSpace, a DBA of On-Demand Publishing, LLC

Disclaimer

This book is designed to provide accurate, authoritative information about mortgages, short sales, and foreclosure. However, no guide or book can ever be entirely complete and comprehensive, and each homeowner's individual financial situation is unique. Homeowners who are considering any major decision with respect to their home are urged to seek legal and financial advice.

Furthermore, the housing market is constantly changing, as are government and lender initiatives for both home-retention programs (such as loan modifications) and home-forfeiture programs (such as short sales). While the information presented here is accurate as this book goes to press, some of the information contained herein may change with time.

This book is distributed with the understanding that neither the authors nor the publisher are rendering legal, tax or financial advice. Homeowners considering a short sale or any other financial decision should seek individual advice appropriate to their personal situation from competent industry professionals, including attorneys, real estate agents, accountants, and financial and tax advisors.

Table of Contents

THE ARK LAW GROUP

COMPLETE GUIDE

to

SHORT SALES

Background

In the four years following the beginning of what is now known as "the financial crisis," from early 2007 to the beginning of 2012, four million American families lost their homes to foreclosure. But the bad news did not stop there. The number of foreclosures continued to rise through much of 2012. By mid-2012, over 10 million borrowers were "underwater" - in other words, their homes were worth less than what they owed on their mortgages. Selling wasn't even an option - at least not through a traditional home sale. And recovery was still not in sight. How did we arrive at this?

The answer comes down mainly to greed: greed on the part of investors looking to make a quick buck, and greed on the part of lenders who engaged in "predatory lending practices" by offering easy money to eager homebuyers. These terms were considered to be "predatory" because they enticed new borrowers with lending terms that were easy to repay at first, but that meant that these borrowers would not likely be able to fulfill their repayment obligations only a few years down the road.

The roots of the financial crisis go back to the early 2000s, when housing prices began to rise rapidly. Between 2000 and 2006, average home prices nearly doubled. With real estate appreciating by 10 to 25% per year, it was natural that almost anyone who thought they could qualify for a mortgage would want to get into the market. In particular, young couples and families thinking about purchasing their first home worried that if they didn't buy then, they might never be able to afford to get in. The pressure was on!

But the profits were not only to be made by buying real estate. The mortgage lenders themselves started to compete for both market share and revenue. Back then, the lending market was strongly influenced by the conservative underwriting practices of the Government Sponsored Enterprises (GSEs): mainly the Federal Home Loan Mortgage Corporation (FHLMC), known as Freddie Mac, and the Federal National Mortgage Association (FNMA), known as Fannie Mae. Mortgage lenders (mostly banks), as the originators of mortgages, packaged up their loans and sold them to the big securitizers: mainly Freddie and Fannie. The banks had to follow the GSE's conservative guidelines, so they were able to offer mortgages only to borrowers who met the GSE's strict lending criteria.

But around 2003, private securitizers began to appear. They wanted in on the profits, too, and they started to buy up loans originated by the banks, generating competition for Freddie and Fannie. More and more Americans wanted to get in on the rising housing market, and more and more lenders wanted to give their money to them. This led to a drop in qualifying standards. Now loans were being issued to what were formerly considered to be "risky" borrowers, who never would have qualified for a loan under the GSE's guidelines: those with no money to put down as a deposit, or those whose income was not high enough to support normal monthly mortgage payments.

With the new investors on board, suddenly lenders had products to offer these risky borrowers. Home loans were available with zero money down. Homeowners could take out a first mortgage for 80% of the purchase price, and a second mortgage for the remaining 20%. They didn't worry, because property prices were rising so quickly; they believed that they would be able to sell at a profit in a couple of years.

Home loans were offered with "teaser" interest rates, such as 2%. The loan would reset to a higher rate, such as 6%, after two or three years. Many of those adjustable-rate mortgages (ARMs) were even offered with an optional payment plan (Opt-ARMSs). Borrowers did not even have to make their full mortgage payments for the first two or three years; they could pay only the interest component of the monthly mortgage payment (or sometimes even less).

The financial industry had once had a checks and balances system. People used to have to qualify for a mortgage, so that the lender would have a high degree of confidence that the borrowers would be able to repay that mortgage. But now, lenders were giving money away (the so-called "subprime mortgages") to people who never would have qualified for a loan a few years previously. The majority of subprime loans were issued between 2004 and 2007.

And then the housing bubble burst. By the middle of 2006, housing prices had reached their peak. Of course, no one ever knows that prices are at a high until after they fall; you need the downturn before you can look back to see where the peak was. However, by August, 2006, it was clear that home prices were beginning to fall. In March, 2007, after months of small declines, home prices suddenly took a tumble: the steepest monthly drop seen in nearly two decades. And from there they continued to plummet, to a low two years later, in 2009, to average values not seen since 2003.

By the end of 2006, foreclosures were already on the rise. The first wave of foreclosures did not affect occupant homeowners so much. The foreclosed-upon owners were mainly real estate investors and speculators who saw real estate prices dropping, and who gave up their properties.

But the second foreclosure wave, hitting around 2008, affected millions of American homeowners. This was a result of those subprime mortgages, as those attractive "teaser" interest rates that were offered in 2005 and 2006 began to reset to the higher rates, meaning substantially higher monthly payments. In addition, borrowers who had been on the "interest-only" option now also had to come up with their full monthly payment. For many Americans, the new monthly payments were more than their household income could afford.

But this was now 2008. Selling was no longer an option, because home prices were 20 to 50% lower than they had been at their peak in 2006. Many of these homeowners had put little or no down payment on their home purchase: their homes were now worth far less than they owed on their mortgages. They were underwater. While a few of these distressed homeowners were able to find solutions through programs such as loan modification or through a short sale, many of them lost their homes through foreclosure.

This second round of foreclosures created entire neighborhoods littered with vacant and unmaintained homes. It also created a glut of REO (bank-owned) properties that flooded the market. So property prices dropped even further, while the economy continued to sputter. Companies down-sized, and laid off staff or cut hours or cut overtime pay. Families' incomes were reduced.

Back in mid-2007, the national unemployment rate had been under 4.5%. By 2010 it was hovering near 10%. Suddenly, people who had had decent credit ratings, who had planned and spent responsibly, who had always paid their mortgage on time, were unable to meet their monthly expenses. The continuing drops in property prices meant that these people became victims of the third wave of foreclosures.

Many tried to keep up their mortgage payments by paying them with their credit cards, hoping that the financial crisis would resolve itself soon. Others chewed away at their investments and retirement savings to avoid defaulting on their mortgage. And others simply defaulted, making the choice that it was more important to put food on the family table, and ensure that there was heat and water in their home.

But the financial crisis has not resolved itself. Although housing prices recovered slightly in late 2009 and early 2010, that was only temporary. Through 2011 they continued to fall, and by early 2012 they had dropped to values even lower than the rock-bottom prices they had hit in early 2009.

So the third foreclosure wave spun off the previous two. Now, even people who had always spent responsibly were losing their homes. Circumstances beyond their control meant that their income had been reduced and they could no longer afford monthly mortgage payments. The dropping property values also meant that they could not sell their homes for what was owed.

For many homeowners across the nation, these national and global circumstances have resulted in losing their homes to foreclosure. However, today there are more alternatives available for homeowners who wish to avoid foreclosure than there were back in 2008 or 2010. This book explores one of those alternatives: the short sale.

Chapter 1

What Are Short Sales And Why Would I Use One?

What Is A Short Sale?

A short sale literally means a home sale where the proceeds from the sale fall "short" of the balance owing on the liens against the property. These liens normally comprise a first mortgage (used to purchase the home or to finance against it). They also may include second or third mortgages, and any other liens such as judgment liens or overdue Homeowners Association fees.

A short sale is normally considered when the homeowner is "underwater" - in other words when they owe more on their home (total of mortgages and other liens) than the current market value of their home. However, in order to obtain "marketable title," a requirement by any lending institution before offering a purchase loan to a new buyer, any liens on the home must be released before title is transferred. This means that an underwater homeowner must get permission from their mortgage lender to sell the home (unless they can come up with the cash at closing to make up the difference between the sales price and the balance owing on the mortgage and other liens plus closing costs). A short sale may also be necessary even when a borrower is not strictly underwater, if they do not have enough equity in their home to pay off the closing costs of the sale.

For example, if a borrower owes $200,000 on their mortgage, and receives a purchase offer for $210,000, they would likely still need their lender's approval to proceed with the sale as a short sale. This is because the closing costs of the sale (agents' commissions, legal fees, outstanding utilities or tax bills, etc.) would likely total around $25,000. The buyer's offer of $210,000 is not sufficient to pay back the $200,000 mortgage plus the $25,000 closing costs. The net proceeds to the lender, deducting the closing costs from the sales price, come to $185,000, which is $15,000 short of the $200,000 balance owing.

The Difference Between A Short Sale And A Pre-Foreclosure Sale

The terms short sale and pre-foreclosure are often used interchangeably. The difference between them is that a pre-foreclosure sale is a short sale by a borrower who is delinquent on their mortgage payments and facing foreclosure. But a short sale can also refer to a sale by a borrower who is not delinquent, where the lender agrees to a payoff that is less than the balance owing on the mortgage.

So a pre-foreclosure sale is a specific class of short sale, where the seller is facing foreclosure. However, in general, the term "short sale" is more widely used, and "pre-foreclosure sale" is used mainly with respect to FHA loans.

A short sale that is not a pre-foreclosure sale could occur, for example, when a borrower realizes that if they do not get rid of the home, they soon will be become delinquent. A short sale can be a preventative action: for example, when a homeowner's income has dropped due to reduced work hours, and they initiate a short sale before they are threatened with foreclosure. See Section 3.4: Strategic Default, below, for more information.

Financial Distress: Using A Short Sale To Avoid Foreclosure

An underwater mortgage does not necessarily mean that you *must* short sale your home. If you want to keep your underwater home, you must have sufficient income to continue making your payments while you wait for your home's value to rise again. But if you are not confident that you can afford to do that, and if you don't take any other action, you may be steering yourself down the road to foreclosure.

Many Americans who are underwater with their mortgages are already struggling to make their mortgage payments. For some, their financial distress is a result of wage cuts or unemployment, or. For others, it may be because of increased living costs due to separation or divorce, or to unexpected debts such as medical bills.

Some homeowners are already behind on their mortgage payments, and foreclosure looms close in their future. Others are still current on their mortgage but know that they do not have the resources to continue making payments for years as they wait for the economy to turn around. Although they are not being threatened by foreclosure yet, they know that they are at risk, and want to be proactive.

A short sale is one option that homeowners can choose, in order to strategically take control of their finances, rather than simply wait for their lender to foreclose on them. (Other options are discussed below, in Chapter 4: What are the alternatives to a short sale?). By choosing a short sale, distressed homeowners can avoid both the stress and stigma of being foreclosed upon, and the black mark that foreclosure brings to their credit score.

Strategic Default

Many homeowners become delinquent on their mortgage payments because they simply do not have enough money to pay all of their bills each month. However, some homeowners actually choose to default on their mortgages. This is called a "strategic default."

Strategic default works by making the borrower's problem the lender's problem. Lenders do not have much incentive to work with a borrower who makes their mortgage payments on time. Why would they? This is their ideal borrower!

However, once a borrower defaults on their mortgage, the lender has a problem: what they call a "non-performing loan." They no longer have a reliable borrower; they have a borrower who doesn't seem to care whether they repay their mortgage or not. Suddenly the lender has to figure out the math. Instead of profiting from the interest on the loan, they now have to work out how to cut their losses. Which option will see them lose less: foreclosing on the borrower (a costly process that may take a year or more to complete) or taking a calculated loss right now by approving a short sale?

In many cases, the lender loses far less via a short sale. Lenders don't want to repossess homes, and then market them and sell them. When faced with the choice of foreclosing on a delinquent borrower or approving a short sale, more and more lenders are choosing the short sale.

The ideal case for a non-delinquent borrower who wants to do a short sale is to convince their lender that they are "at imminent risk of default." This means that, although they are current on mortgage payments right now, their financial situation (e.g. reduced income, increased expenses) means that they foresee that they will soon be forced to default on their mortgage payments. If a short sale can be completed without delinquency on mortgage payments, the hit to the borrower's credit score will be minimal.

Some lenders will talk at this stage, but others will not look at the case until the borrower is already delinquent. If that is the case, some borrowers choose a "strategic default," in order to open up the conversation.

Doesn't All My Private Information Get Shared If I Attempt A Short Sale?

Well, not "all" of your private information. But yes, you must disclose (or share) your financial information in order to work in good faith on the short sale process.

This is one part of the short sale process that makes some homeowners nervous. But if you think of a short sale as a negotiation between two parties: the person who owes money on a mortgage loan, and the lender who is considering forgiving a portion of the debt owing, it makes sense.

A short sale means that the lender is agreeing to take a loss on the money that they loaned. So it only makes sense that they need full access to the borrower's financial information, in order to decide whether they are willing to take that loss. If the borrower has money stashed away in savings accounts or other investments, the lender will likely (and probably fairly) reject the short sale request or ask for a cash contribution.

In order for a lender to assess that a borrower genuinely cannot afford to continue paying their mortgage - for whatever reason - the lender needs to see proof of the borrower's financial situation. This normally means providing records such as: bank account statements to show assets, pay stubs to show proof of income, and information regarding monthly expenses such as bills and car payments.

Your lender will normally ask to see your previous 60 days of bank account statements. Investors Fannie Mae and Freddie Mac have a savings account threshold for requesting a cash contribution of $10,000. This means that if the investor on your loan is Freddie or Fannie (which would encompass most, but not all, mortgage loans), and your lender sees records in that 60-day period that you hold in savings of over $10,000, your lender will likely ask you for a cash contribution in addition to the short sale proceeds.

Why Would A Lender Approve A Short Sale And Accept Less Than Owing?

As partially covered in Section 3.4: Strategic default, above, the lender's main goal (like that of any business) is to make money. Failing that, their goal is to lose as little as possible.

Non-performing mortgages, those mortgages where a borrower is delinquent on their monthly mortgage payments, represent a loss to the lender. Once a mortgage is categorized as "non-performing," the lender's aim is no longer to make money. It is just to lose as little money as possible. This is called "loss mitigation."

A lender will look at both the borrower's hardship (for example, loss of income or increased expenses, spelled out in a letter: see Section 12.8: How do I write a convincing hardship letter?). But even more important in their decision-making process is doing some simple math. How much will they lose: approving a short sale now, versus foreclosing on a home, and paying all of the associated legal costs, and selling that home at some unknown price at some unknown date in the future?

"Loss mitigation" is not about making profit; it is about minimizing loss. At the moment, short sales are surging. This is in part because more homeowners are realizing that a short sale is a viable and realistic option that will protect them from foreclosure. But even more, it is because lenders are realizing that short sales are an effective strategy for their own loss mitigation. If they approve a short sale now, they take a quick but finite loss to get themselves out of a non-performing mortgage. However, if they don't approve a short sale, they will have to take legal action to gain possession of the home, and spend money to refurbish it and market it as an REO (real-estate owned) property.

Once you account for the time delays involved in foreclosure and then marketing of an REO property, not to mention associated legal fees and broker fees, foreclosure can be a costly option for a lender. And this is exactly why your lender may elect to approve a short sale - even though it means taking a loss.

Why Would I Choose A Short Sale, When I Am Not Getting Anything Out Of It?

One reason to choose a short sale over foreclosure is to preserve your credit rating. A second reason is for your long-term financial stability, and not to continue putting money into a sinking ship. A final reason is to preserve your dignity: to avoid the stigma that having your lender foreclose upon you brings.

A short sale scars your credit rating far less than having a foreclosure on your record does. Foreclosure hits credit scores hard, generally costing 200 to 300 points. Short sales can cost as little as 50 to 100 points, or even less, especially if the homeowner has been able to remain current on mortgage payments. (See Section 6.5: Credit score and credit report, for more information).

Even if you are not facing imminent foreclosure, a short sale can be a strategic move to unburden yourself from debt. Perhaps you have been able to keep up on your mortgage payments so far. But if your house is worth less than what you owe (and probably will be so for years to come), and you are not confident that you will be able to continue making the mortgage payments, there may not be much good reason to keep sinking money into it. You may not get any money out of your home by conducting a short sale - but at least you are not putting more money into a losing investment.

For example, if a house with a $2,500/month mortgage payment is going to be underwater for seven years, that would represent a total of $210,000 in mortgage payments to the lender over that time. However, if that house were to be sold now, instead, and the sellers moved to less expensive housing with a monthly cost of $1,500/month and banked the savings, they would end up with $84,000 in savings. A short sale is not a way to make money, but it is a very effective way to cut losses.

Another reason to choose a short sale over foreclosure is simply for feelings of self-worth. For many homeowners, it is more empowering to choose an outcome, to choose to negotiate a short payoff with a lender and to close that deal, than it is to allow yourself to be a passive victim and simply await the lender to foreclose upon you.

And then there also is the stigma of foreclosure: of having friends and family and neighbors know that you did not pay your debts and that your lender repossessed your home. A short sale represents a dignified exit from a bad mortgage, a way for a homeowner to work with a lender to find an outcome that is negotiated and agreed upon by both parties.

Chapter 2

What Are My Alternatives To A Short Sale?

This book focuses upon the short sale as a viable alternative to foreclosure. However, there are other options available to distressed homeowners, and it is important that you investigate all options before arriving at a decision of what is best for you.

Renting Out The Property

Renting out a home to cover the mortgage payments may be one way to keep a home. This may work for people who have been transferred due to employment but who do not want to sell because they are underwater with their mortgage. This may also work for homeowners who can find rental accommodation where their rent is substantially cheaper than the rent they charge for the home they own.

The reality, however, in today's market, is that few homes will rent out for more than what the monthly mortgage payments are. Most homeowners will still have to pay every month to "top up" those mortgage payments - as well as pay the monthly mortgage or rent in the home they are living in. Homeowners who are thinking of renting their home out must also take into account that the home may be vacant at times, and that renters may not take care of it the same way that owners do: there may be more repair bills.

Renting a property out may work provided that the rent you take in more than covers the mortgage payments, or if you have the cash to top up the mortgage payments until property prices rise enough that you can sell at a profit - keeping in mind that this could take many years.

Refinance

Refinancing a mortgage means replacing the existing mortgage with a new loan. This involves paying off an existing mortgage, and creating a new one. Normally, the borrower will have to qualify for refinancing in exactly the same way that they qualify for a new mortgage: there must be enough equity in the property used to secure the lien to satisfy the lender's standards, and the borrower must have a good credit rating and meet minimum income standards.

Reasons to refinance are usually to get a lower interest rate, or to get a mortgage with more favorable terms, such as offering a fixed interest rate rather than an adjustable rate, or changing the term of the mortgage. A longer term will mean lower monthly payments, and may be more attractive to borrowers who are struggling to make payments. But a shorter term means you pay off the loan sooner, saving thousands and dollars of interest overall, and will be more desirable for borrowers looking out for their long-term financial health.

Refinancing can also be used to combine mortgages. For example, if there is both a first and second mortgage on a home, these could be combined into one new loan.

Although refinancing can save a borrower money by negotiating better mortgage terms, refinancing comes at a cost. The total cost to refinance usually come to between 3 and 6 per cent of the outstanding principal on the loan. Set costs include application, loan origination, appraisal, inspection and attorney fees and title search, and there also may be "points fees" of up to 3% of the loan principal. Some loans also charge a "prepayment penalty" of between one and six months' interest payments for paying out the mortgage early. So, if a borrower owes $200,000, their refinancing cost would likely be between $6,000 and $12,000. This cost must be weighed against the eventual savings through the refinancing, to see if it is worth going through the whole process.

Refinancing is not available to borrowers who are underwater with their mortgages, or close to it, as they will not have the equity in their property to qualify for the new mortgage. Refinancing is also not usually available to borrowers who are already struggling to make mortgage payments due to reduced income or increased living expenses because they will probably not meet the lender's minimum income requirements to qualify for a loan.

Loan Modification

This is the option that many borrowers who do not qualify for refinancing will try next.

A loan modification is a permanent adjustment made to one or more of the terms of a borrower's existing loan. The aim of a loan modification is to bring the delinquent mortgage current, and to give the borrower a new start at making payments that they can afford.

Lenders are unlikely to reduce the total balance owing on the loan. Usually, a loan modification will involve dropping the interest rate, in order to make monthly payments more affordable. It often will also involve extending the term of the loan. While this lowers monthly payments, it also results in the borrower paying many thousands of dollars in extra interest over the term of the loan.

Most homeowners seeking a loan modification are already behind on their monthly mortgage payments. In a loan modification, the new monthly payments often include an amount to gradually make up for previously missed payments. So, in many loan modifications, the new monthly payments actually end up being higher than they were before, putting already-distressed borrowers at a high risk of defaulting again soon.

The federal government introduced a loan modification program called Home Affordable Modification Program (HAMP) in early 2009. The aim of the program was to help American homeowners negotiate loan modifications so they could keep their homes and avoid foreclosure. HAMP was originally predicted to assist between 3 and 4 million homeowners by creating guidelines by which lenders could work with homeowners to modify their loans, so that both lenders and borrowers could avoid the losses to both sides that foreclosure brings.

However, HAMP is now widely regarded as a failure. Many of the trial modification never made their way to becoming permanent modifications. And a high number of the permanent modifications re-defaulted within 12 months.

Loan modifications can help homeowners who are dedicated to remaining in their houses, and who know they will have the means to keep making their mortgage payments on the new payment plan.

However, the loan modification process has ended up with tragic results for many American homeowners. Some homeowners who were making their modification payments on time were inexplicably denied a permanent modification by their lender - and then told that they must make up the difference between their regular payments and the discounted payments. Many others became submerged in tales of repeatedly lost paperwork by their lenders, reapplying and resubmitting forms as they got more and more behind on their loans. And many who were approved for loan modifications simply could not afford the new payments, and found themselves in default again.

The tragic aspect of this result is that all of the homeowners who attempted a loan modification but failed lost valuable time. While attempting the loan modification, they were either sinking more money into their house or becoming more delinquent on payments. And all the while, the prices of their homes continued to fall. For many, by the time they realized that a loan modification was not going to work for them, it was too late to take any other action. They were too behind on payments, or their property value had sunk too low, to attempt any other actions such as a short sale. All they could do was await foreclosure.

Forbearance

Forbearance is a temporary suspension or reduction of loan payments. A lender will probably only grant forbearance if the hardship causing the borrower to miss payments is temporary, and if there were no missed mortgage payments prior to that hardship. Examples of temporary hardships could be loss of income due to a medical condition, or costs resulting from a natural disaster. Usually, a lender will want to see that there is an end in sight to that temporary hardship, such as a date when the borrower will return to work, or when an insurance payment to cover living expenses following the natural disaster will be received. Lenders may grant forbearance due to unemployment, if the borrower is actively looking for work.

Forbearance will usually only be granted for periods of three to twelve months. At the end of the forbearance period, i.e. when that temporary hardship is relieved, the borrower will be expected to make up all of the missed payments, either by paying them out or through a repayment plan.

Repayment Plan

A repayment is just what its name suggests: coming up with a payment schedule to make up for missed mortgage payments. It is similar to forbearance, in that a lender is unlikely to approve it unless the reason that the borrower got behind on payments is due to a temporary hardship, such as unemployment, or a death in the family, that is now past.

A lender is unlikely to approve a repayment plan unless they have convincing evidence that the borrower can make those repayments. The repayment plan payments are added on top of the regular mortgage payments until the overdue amounts have been paid out. Repayment plans usually do not involve changing any of the terms of the mortgage.

Deed In Lieu (DIL)

A Deed in Lieu of Foreclosure is also known as voluntary foreclosure: the homeowner voluntarily transfers the deed of the property to the lender. This is generally a last resort plan, if all other options have failed. Its only value over foreclosure is that is saves the stress of having to go through the whole foreclosure process, and that the hit to the borrower's credit score <u>may</u> be less than that of a foreclosure (although some lenders may report a DIL as a foreclosure to the credit bureau).

To complete a DIL, the keys must be handed over to the lender, who will conduct a property inspection. For the DIL to be accepted, the lender will expect the property to be clean and free of debris, and that items such as light fixtures and appliances have not been removed.

A borrower who is completing a DIL should make sure that the lender provides a written deficiency waiver, stating that they will not pursue the borrower for any unpaid balance on the mortgage.

Do Nothing. (Wait For Foreclosure)

Taking no action: not making mortgage payments, and not communicating with your lender, will lead to foreclosure. To some homeowners, this would seem to be the option with the least stress, because they don't have to do anything, and they can live in the home for free until the day that the sheriff finally boots them out. However, to other homeowners, this would be the most stressful option of all: receiving notices and fielding phone calls from the lender, then either walking away and finding new accommodation or living in the home knowing at some point they will be tossed out. Not to mention the stigma: having notices posted on your home, and having friends and family members know you have been foreclosed upon.

The exact way that the foreclosure process proceeds varies from state to state. (See Chapter 5: Mortgages and Foreclosure, and Appendices B and C, for more information). However, the general procedure is that once a borrower has missed two or so payments, the lender will begin to send letters demanding payment and threatening to start the foreclosure process.

If the borrower does not respond to those demands, and does not make any payments, eventually a sale date for the home will be set. A borrower may reinstate the mortgage before that sale date by making up all overdue payments and penalties. If they do not reinstate the mortgage, the property will be sold at auction to the highest bidder.

The foreclosure process follows fairly set timelines, and normally the whole process takes under a year. However, in some cases lenders do not even initiate the process for years.

Borrowers who choose to go through with the foreclosure process do not have to do anything. They can occupy the home until it is sold, when, if they have not already moved out, they will be evicted by the sheriff. However, homeowners who find themselves being foreclosed upon against their will can take steps to slow down the foreclosure process while they investigate other options, or even stop foreclosure all together: take a look at Section 5.10: How can you slow or stop the process once started?

Bankruptcy

All of the solutions above (other than renting the property out) give a lot of power to your lender: the lender is the one who initiates or approves what happens. Bankruptcy is the one financial solution that you can choose for yourself. Although lenders can, theoretically, force you into involuntary bankruptcy, in practice this is not in their interest, and it happens only in extremely rare circumstances.

Generally, a lender cannot impose bankruptcy on you, and they have no say in your decision to declare bankruptcy.

Bankruptcy can carry a stigma with it, and it is not for everyone. However, anyone in financial distress and fearful that they may lose their home should investigate all options open to them, including bankruptcy, before coming to any decisions.

Many homeowners who are in debt are honest people who only want to clear their name and get a fresh start. Declaring bankruptcy is a way of assessing a financial situation and taking charge of it. While many people fear bankruptcy because they believe it means they will lose everything, bankruptcy can allow for exempting assets, including equity in the family home, and in many cases people who declare bankruptcy don't lose anything at all.

Declaring bankruptcy can stop a foreclosure outright. In Chapter 7 bankruptcy, if a homeowner's equity in their home is below a certain amount, they may be able to exempt their home from the bankruptcy: in other words, keep it. This equity amount varies state by state; current information regarding each state is available at http://www.legalconsumer.com/bankruptcy/laws/. The home remains outside of the bankruptcy, the homeowner continues to make mortgage payments, and the bankruptcy is used to deal with other unsecured debts, such as credit cards and auto loans - thereby making mortgage payments more manageable.

Chapter 13 bankruptcy stops the foreclosure process long enough for the borrower to negotiate a repayment plan with the lender for missed payments, or to attempt to negotiate a loan modification or a short sale with their lender.

One advantage of bankruptcy is that it deals not only with mortgage debt, it deals with all debts. Most homeowners who are struggling to pay their mortgages also have other debts that they are having trouble paying: credit cards, car loans, etc. Bankruptcy creates a plan for dealing with all of the debts - often wiping many of them out completely.

Bankruptcy can also be used in conjunction with some of the other strategies mentioned above. See Chapter 18: Bankruptcy and short sales.

While bankruptcy is not for everyone, declaring bankruptcy should be considered by any distressed homeowner who is looking to get their finances in order - whether in conjunction with other strategies such as a short sale, or on its own. For many, bankruptcy is the fastest and most direct way to put old debts behind and to get a fresh financial start.

How To Choose What Is Right For You

There are a lot of potential solutions for distressed homeowners! There is no right solution for everyone. The "right" solution will depend upon the specific details of your financial situation, your lender's willingness to problem-solve and negotiate, and even on your own personality.

It is important that you review all of the information you can about all of your options - but also that you seek professional advice. You should seek the professional advice of accountants, attorneys who specialize in real estate and in bankruptcy, as well as real estate professionals. You may need to hire several individuals, but you may also find companies where these professionals work together as a team. You need to find the solution that works best for you, and you also need to know if there are any longer-term implications of the decisions you make now. For example, if you get rid of the house through foreclosure or a short sale, might you still be responsible to pay back part of the debt to your lender years down the road? Or, if some of your debt has been forgiven, will you be required to pay income tax on that forgiven debt?

Do everything you can to become properly informed. This means research and reading, and it also means working with industry professionals who can provide you with the best personal advice.

Why Bother Doing Anything - My Credit Is Ruined Anyway?

Financial troubles cause stress. Doing nothing will not make the problem, or the stress, go away. That is the most important reason to deal with an underwater mortgage.

Some people have the type of personality where they can sit back and do nothing, ignoring creditor calls and demands for payment, and somehow not get stressed by the uncertainty. However, most people feel much better about themselves once they get informed, start making some decisions for themselves, and take action. Getting started may be difficult: it takes some energy and motivation to start finding out what the options are, and doing some research and making some phone calls. But the fact that you are reading this book shows that you have already taken that first, difficult step in getting your financial affairs in order.

There are many other reasons to take action, too. One of the foremost is to preserve what you can of your credit rating. As explained below, in Section 6.5, the hit to your credit score may be substantially worse from foreclosure (200 to 300 points) than from a short sale (50 to 100 points, possibly even less). Although things might seem dire right now, in a few years you may want to purchase a new home, or get a car loan, or perhaps secure lower interest rates on your credit card. Simply doing nothing guarantees foreclosure. Taking action to avoid foreclosure can keep you from getting that stain on your credit rating.

Another important reason to do something is simply how you feel about the outcome. A mortgage loan constitutes an obligation you made to your lender: you promised to repay that loan. Not repaying that loan, and ignoring your lender, is not a solution that many borrowers will feel proud of. Taking charge and communicating with your lender to try to find a mutually agreeable solution is a way to walk out of a difficult situation with dignity.

Chapter 3

Mortgages And Foreclosure: How Do They Work?

What Is A Mortgage?

There are actually two different ways that the word "mortgage" is used these days, and that can sometimes make things confusing.

A "mortgage loan" is a loan taken out for the purchase of "real property" (real estate), and it actually consists of two parts: the promissory note ("Note") and the security interest ("Deed of Trust" or "Mortgage" depending upon which state you live in). The Note is your promise to repay your lender the money you have borrowed. The Mortgage is a contract pledging the property as collateral for the loan and is recorded in the public records of the county in which the property is located. The borrower transfers their interest in the property to the lender or to a trustee (in a Deed of Trust state), on the understanding that that ownership interest will be transferred back to them once the terms of the loan have been satisfied. If the borrower defaults on the Note, the lender uses the power of sale in the Mortgage to foreclose upon and take possession of the property. The Mortgage is attached to the property, not to the borrower - so even if the borrower transfers the property to someone else, the mortgagee (lender) still has the right to take possession of the property if the borrower does not pay back the loan.

Although the word Mortgage strictly refers to the security interest, today, most people use the word "mortgage" to refer to the whole mortgage loan: both the promise to repay, and the security interest or lien. And that is how we will use the word "mortgage" in this book. However, it is very important to pay attention to the strict use of the word "mortgage" when it comes to wording regarding deficiencies when a lender approves a short sale. If a lender releases only the mortgage, meaning just the lien, the borrower may still be responsible to repay the note in full. See Chapter 14: Deficiency balance for more detailed information.

How Mortgages Work

First, a potential borrower has to qualify for a mortgage. This means that they must provide information to convince a lender that they will be able to repay the mortgage loan.

Information a borrower usually will have to provide a lender includes:

- financial information, regarding existing debts and assets

- evidence about ability to pay and cash flow: how much money they earn, and what their monthly expenses are

- references of their past record of repaying debts, provided via their credit score and credit report

- information about the property they intend to purchase: that the purchase price represents fair market value, so the lender can calculate the "loan-to-value" ratio.

If the lender approves the loan, they will spell out the terms of the mortgage. The terms include the interest rate, and the amortization period, which is how many years it will take to pay off the loan. If the loan is for more than 80% of the purchase price, the loan is considered to be more risky, and they will require the borrower to purchase mortgage insurance.

There are different ways that a lender may calculate and charge interest. Borrowers with high credit scores generally qualify for lower interest rates. Borrowers who are considered "risky" by the lender are charged higher interest rates, to offset the higher risk that the lender is taking. Interest may be calculated as a fixed annual rate, for example 4% per year. Or, interest may be charged at an adjustable rate.

Many mortgages offered in the mid-2000s were adjustable-rate mortgages (ARMs) meant to entice new borrowers with low interest rates such as 2%, that would reset to higher rates such as 6% after two or three years. Another, less common type of adjustable-rate mortgage is a floating-rate mortgage (also called variable-rate mortgage), where the interest may fluctuate according to some base rate, or at the lender's discretion.

The amortization period is how long it will take to pay off the loan. It, and the interest rate, are used to calculate how much the monthly payments must be. Amortization periods are typically between fifteen and thirty years. The longer the amortization period is, the lower the monthly payments will be - because you have so many more months to pay off the loan. However, by taking five or ten extra years to pay off the loan, the total amount of interest paid by the end of the loan may come to tens of thousands of dollars more. Borrowers who are having trouble making their monthly mortgage payments may be offered a loan modification that extends the amortization period. While this may solve their cash flow problems temporarily, this can prove to be a very expensive long-term solution.

Lenders such as banks often sell their mortgages to investors. In this case, the investor becomes the owner of the loan, but the lender who gave you the loan will still do any paperwork or administration related to the loan: they remain as servicer of the loan.

Types Of Mortgages

Mortgages can be classified by how risky the lender perceives the borrower. Here is a brief primer on how mortgages are classified:

- **Conforming mortgages (also called "standard mortgages").** These are mortgages that meet the fairly conservative rules and guidelines established by the GSEs Freddie Mac and Fannie Mae.

- **Nonconforming mortgages.** These are mortgages that do not meet the GSE guidelines. As discussed above, they became common in the mid-2000s as more private investors moved in to take part in the booming mortgage industry by dropping the qualifying standards for loans.

- **A-loan (or "prime loan"):** A mortgage loan to a highly qualified, low-risk borrower. Typically, this requires a credit score of 700 or higher.

- **Alt-A loan:** Formerly, this was a mortgage loan to a borrower who came close to meeting the A-loan standard, with a credit score in the high 600s. Now, loans that do quite not meet other criteria of an A-loan may also be considered Alt-A loans. For example, if the borrower does not have documentation to support their stated income, or if the loan-to-value ratio is too high.

- **Subprime loan:** A mortgage loan to a borrower who does not meet the usual lending criteria. A decade or so ago, this type of borrower would probably never be approved for a mortgage at all. But, with the lax lending standards of the mid-2000s, peaking in 2004-2007, subprime mortgages were being approved by the thousands.

How Liens Work

A lien is a security interest in a property meant to ensure the repayment of a debt. It is the collateral that secures a debt.

The most common kind of lien is the lien securing a promissory note. A mortgage lien is a "consensual" lien - where the borrower agrees to transfer their interest in the property to the lender or a trustee, with the understanding that that interest will be transferred back to the borrower once the loan has been repaid. It is the lender's security that the borrower <u>will</u> pay back the money.

There are also "nonconsensual" liens. These may be placed upon a property without the owner's consent, to secure repayment of a debt. Examples include tax liens for unpaid taxes, mechanic's liens for unpaid bills for work done on property or land, and judgment liens from other debts (placed by other creditors via a legal judgment). Also, in most developments managed by a Homeowners Association (HOA), the HOA has the right to place a lien on the property if the owner becomes delinquent on their HOA dues or fees.

Liens are attached to the actual property, not to the property's owner. They are registered against the home (where they must be registered varies state by state); anyone who conducts a title search on a property will find out what liens are registered against it. So if the homeowner/debtor transfers the property to someone else, those liens will become the responsibility of that new owner.

For this reason, it is difficult, or more likely impossible, to sell a home with liens on it. A new purchaser will conduct a title search on the property, so they know what they are getting into. They will not likely take on a property that has debts associated with it. And, more importantly, they will probably not be able to get financing for the purchase, because lenders will not typically finance a home that already has liens associated with it.

The "first lien" is almost always associated with the mortgage used to purchase the home. There may also be a second mortgage taken out to purchase the home, with a "second lien," or a Home Equity Line of Credit (HELOC) taken out against the home at a later date that represents a second or third or even fourth lien. Finally, there may be other liens, such as judgment liens or HOA liens. Although most homes only have one or two liens recorded, it is possible for some homes to have four or five or more liens - all of which must be released in order for the property to change hands: what is known as "marketable title."

Liens work within the framework of priority lien status, usually in the order that they are recorded. If a property is sold, the funds go to pay out the first lien-holder. If there are funds to spare, they pay the second lien-holder. If there are still funds to spare, they go to the third, and so on. If there are not enough funds to satisfy one lien-holder, all of the others with lower priority (more junior liens) get nothing.

There are some exceptions to the chronological priority of liens. The most common exception is for tax liens: if the lien-holder is a state taxing body, their liens usually supersede any of the other liens. Some states also give "super-priority lien" status to HOA liens or Condominium Owners Association liens, where those liens may take priority over other liens provided that certain conditions are met; check your own state regulations.

Any of the lien-holders may foreclose upon the homeowner. However, in today's economic climate, nearly all foreclosures are initiated by the first lien-holder. This is because so many homes are "underwater." They are not worth enough to even pay out the first lien-holder - which means that there is no point in a junior lien-holder initiating a foreclosure: they won't get anything out of it.

However, if a more senior lien-holder threatens foreclosure, but the case can be moved to a short sale, the junior lien-holder now has a bit of bargaining power: they can ask for some small portion of the sales proceeds (usually a few hundred to a few thousand dollars) in order to approve the sale and release their lien. For second liens attached to second mortgages, this often means that lenders are accepting 10% or less of the balance owing on the mortgage - and they do it, because their alternatives (refusing approval and allowing the property to go to foreclosure, or foreclosing themselves) will net them zero.

The one recourse that junior lenders have, however, is retaining their right to pursue the deficiency balance. Most junior lenders these days waive that right, but it's important to read your approval letter carefully to make sure that you understand exactly what the junior lenders are agreeing to.

Recourse/Non-Recourse Loans, And What This Means For Deficiency

Different states have different laws about mortgages, loans, and foreclosure. Some are "recourse states" and some are "non-recourse states."

In a recourse state, if you default on your secured lender, your lender can not only come after the item that you used to secure your loan (in the case of a mortgage, your home) - they can also pursue you for any deficiency balance or other costs. For example, if you owe $250,000 on your mortgage, and the lender is eventually able to recover $200,000 by seizing and selling your home, the lender has still lost $50,000 in the whole deal. In a recourse state, you still owe them that $50,000, and they can pursue you to recover it.

In a non-recourse state, your lender can only come after the item that you used to secure your loan. So in the example above, the $50,000 deficiency would be the lender's loss, and they cannot hold you responsible for it.

However, the exact regulations are different from state to state, regarding whether a loan is considered non-recourse or not, and whether the borrower may be responsible for a portion of the deficiency balance. Some non-recourse states give non-recourse status only to loans that were used for purchase money: so a second mortgage used to purchase the home would be considered non-recourse, but a second mortgage (HELOC) used for another purpose would be a recourse loan. A few non-recourse states allow the lender to collect a portion of the deficiency balance of the loan, such as the difference between the remaining debt and the current fair market value of the property.

Some recourse states are considered "one-action" states. This rule is to protect borrowers from lenders harassing them with numerous legal actions. It means that the lender has only one opportunity to collect the debt, one single lawsuit: either by foreclosing on the property or by suing the borrower. A lender who forecloses out of court (non-judicially) has taken their one action, and may not later on sue to recover the deficiency. However, if they sue to obtain a foreclosure order (a judicial foreclosure), and the sales proceeds are not enough to cover the mortgage balance owing, then the deficiency judgment for the balance may be included as part of that action.

It is important to note here that a foreclosure is considered an "action" and a short sale is not. Although theoretically a lender in a one-action state could sue for the deficiency balance as their "one action" following a short sale, in reality they are unlikely to do so.

Appendix B lists recourse and non-recourse states. Make sure you look up any regulations specific to your state as well, such as purchase money requirements or whether yours is a one-action state.

Changing Mortgages: About Terminating, Modifying, And Defaulting On Mortgages.

A mortgage is a binding contract between the borrower and lender, usually for a term of between fifteen and thirty years. There will be terms written into the contract about how to terminate the mortgage early, for example if the homeowner wants to sell the property and pay the mortgage out before the term is up. Often those terms will include a "prepayment" penalty, which may be between one and six months of interest payments. This prepayment penalty may also be due if you refinance, since refinancing means terminating the mortgage early to negotiate a new mortgage (see Section 4.2: Refinance, above).

Defaulting on a mortgage is when the borrower does not make the monthly payment that they are supposed to make according to the mortgage contract. Mortgage defaults, or delinquencies, are usually classified as greater than 30 days delinquent, greater than 60 days delinquent, and greater than 90 days delinquent. Lenders may start calling as soon as a payment is late, and they will usually begin to send demand letters for payment once the loan is greater than 30 or 60 days delinquent. They may begin foreclosure proceedings after the loan is greater than 90 days delinquent - although with the backlog in foreclosure in recent years, in some cases it could be a year or more before lenders initiate foreclosure.

What Is Foreclosure?

Foreclosure is a legal process where the lender accesses their right to the security interest they have in a property if the borrower has stopped making their payments on the loan. The lender forces the sale of the asset in order to recover the balance owing on the loan. Since so many homes today are underwater on their mortgages, the foreclosing lender, in most cases, does not recover the full balance owing. Foreclosure becomes a strategy of loss mitigation: cutting losses, but not fully recovering them.

Exactly how the foreclosure process proceeds depends upon whether you are in a judicial or non-judicial state.

The judicial process of foreclosure, which involves filing a lawsuit to obtain a court order to foreclose, is used when no power of sale is present in the mortgage or deed of trust. Generally, after the court declares a foreclosure, the property will be auctioned off to the highest bidder.

The non-judicial process of foreclosure is used when a power of sale clause exists in a mortgage or deed of trust. A "power of sale" clause is the clause in a deed of trust or mortgage in which the borrower pre-authorizes the sale of property to pay off the balance on a loan in the event of their default. In deeds of trust or mortgages where a power of sale clause exists, the power given to the lender to sell the property may be executed by the lender or their representative, typically referred to as the trustee. See Appendix C for a listing of judicial and non-judicial states.

Once a lender has initiated the foreclosure process, a borrower may reinstate the mortgage. The amount of time they have to do this varies state by state. In order to reinstate the mortgage, the borrower must make up all of the money owed to the lender, including all missed payments, all penalties, and any foreclosure costs. This will bring the mortgage back from delinquency into being current again.

How Do You Avoid Foreclosure?

A sure way to avoid foreclosure is to remain current on your mortgage payments. A lender (or other lien-holder) may not foreclose on a borrower who is making their loan payments on time.

However, in today's financial market, remaining current on mortgage payments is not always an option. Many Americans have suffered substantial drops in income, due to having their work hours reduced or to being laid off completely. Many self-employed workers have lost most of their income due to the sluggish economy causing reduced sales or reduced contracts. For some, increased costs, for example unexpected medical bills or expenses resulting from a separation or divorce, have made it difficult to make mortgage payments on time.

So for many, making monthly mortgage payments on time is no longer a choice. But that does not mean that foreclosure is necessarily in the cards. There are many ways of avoiding foreclosure - even once the lender has started the foreclosure process - including the increasingly popular option of a short sale, as well as many other alternatives (outlined in Chapter 4: What are the alternatives to a short sale?)

What is important, though, is acting early. The earlier a struggling homeowner takes action, the more options they will have to exit gracefully from a mortgage that they have no hope of being able to repay. The ideal time to act is, if possible, before they have even defaulted on the mortgage: as soon as they realize that the finances no longer add up and trouble is looming. For some, though, the financial pressure may at first appear temporary, and they will have already defaulted on a few payments before they realize that they can't get out of this on their own and need help. The point is to take action as soon as possible, in order to have as many options for avoiding foreclosure available.

How Does A Bank Foreclose?

The exact foreclosure procedure and timeline varies somewhat state by state. Here is a general overview of the process.

Once you have missed one or two mortgage payments, the lender will begin to send you notices reminding you that you are overdue on your payments. If you make up those missed payments in the first two to three months, and then continue to make your payments on time, they will stop sending you the notices and your mortgage will be current again (however, the late payments may end up noted on your credit report).

If you don't make up the payments, the lender will get more aggressive with their notices, and possibly threaten foreclosure. If you still do not make your payments and do not respond, their attorney will send you a demand letter, formally notifying you that if you do not bring your mortgage current immediately, they will initiate foreclosure proceedings.

If you still don't respond, the lender will issue you with a Notice of Default (NOD), which means they have filed for foreclosure. You can still reinstate your mortgage at this point by paying your lender all outstanding payments, penalties, and foreclosure costs. However, if you do not reinstate the mortgage, the property will be scheduled for sale by auction. The lender, and all other lien-holders, will be repaid what is owing to them, in the order in which the liens were recorded. If there is not enough money to go around, the senior lien-holders are paid out, and the more junior ones get nothing.

The borrower only receives money from the sale if there are funds left over once all liens and foreclosure costs have been paid. (This is very unlikely). Title of the home transfers to the highest bidder at the sale. The borrower no longer has any rights to the property, and must move out.

How Can You Slow Or Stop The Process Once Started?

Just because a lender initiates a foreclosure, does not mean that the case will necessary proceed to foreclosure. There are many ways that you can delay, or even stop, foreclosure proceedings. Delaying foreclosure may be a useful tactic if a homeowner is working to find other solutions, for example to buy time in order to negotiate a short sale.

Reinstatement of mortgage. As indicated above, a homeowner threatened with foreclosure can stop the foreclosure at any time by paying the lender all overdue mortgage payments and penalties, as well the lender's foreclosure costs.

Declaring bankruptcy. The moment a person files for bankruptcy, an "automatic stay" is imposed, which prohibits collection actions, including foreclosure, against the estate. If the homeowner has declared Chapter 7 bankruptcy ("liquidation"), the lender will probably file to request relief from the automatic stay. So filing Chapter 7 bankruptcy usually will delay, but not stop, the foreclosure.

However, Chapter 13 ("reorganization") can stop foreclosure for a longer period of time, or even permanently. Chapter 13 bankruptcy usually allows the homeowner six months to come up with a plan: either work out a repayment plan to make up missed payments with the lender, or negotiate a loan modification, or negotiate a short sale. If the homeowner complies with that plan, foreclosure is stopped for good. If they do not make their payments, the lender can resume the foreclosure proceedings.

Apply for a loan modification. A lender may delay foreclosure proceedings in cases where the mortgage loan is under review for the HAMP loan modification program, or is in an active modification trial plan. If you end up being one of the few who actually does succeed at negotiating an affordable loan-modification, and you meet those payments, the foreclosure will be stopped. If your loan modification is not approved, at least you will have bought some time to investigate other solutions while the application was in progress and the foreclosure proceedings were suspended.

Contest the foreclosure. Unless you are prepared to put in some research into how to contest a motion in court, you will probably need an attorney to contest the foreclosure. With the glut of foreclosures and sloppy paperwork by loan servicers in the past few years, it is reasonably likely that you will discover something the lender did wrong somewhere, and that may form the grounds for you to contest the foreclosure. Since your loan has probably been sold, one avenue to pursue is to contest who owns the original loan.

Wait until the last minute to file paperwork. Once a lawsuit to foreclose has been filed, you will be required to respond to certain actions within a specific amount of time. The lender cannot take their next step until you respond. If you take the maximum time to respond each time - for example, if you are required to respond within 20 days, responding on the 19th day - you will prolong the whole foreclosure process.

Have a short sale in the works. Some lenders will suspend foreclosure proceedings if the borrower informs them that they wish to attempt a short sale. However, even if a lender decides to "dual-track" a file (continue taking steps towards foreclosure even while the short sale package is under review), if there is an interested buyer and the short sale is progressing, the lender will usually agree to postpone the trustee sale date in order to close the short sale.

Request a hearing. If you are in a judicial state (see Appendix C for a list of judicial states) the lender must sue you to initiate the foreclosure process. You will then have a set amount of time to respond (usually around 20 days). If you are in need of extra time - for example, if you are trying to negotiate a short sale - you may respond by requesting a hearing. Even if you do not have a valid reason to stop the foreclosure, and the judge may rule against you at the hearing, the extra time you have bought simply by requesting a hearing (which may take weeks or even months to schedule) may be just what you need in order to get a short sale approved and close on the real estate transaction.

Check your local state regulations. Some states have made recent changes to their state laws regarding foreclosure, for example allowing borrowers to have a chance to attempt mediation before the lender proceeds with the foreclosure. Mediation requires that both parties produce documentation, and that they schedule a meeting with the purpose of finding an alternative to foreclosure - procedures which could take two to three months to complete. It is well worth having an attorney who is familiar with the regulations in your own state to advise you here.

Chapter 4

Foreclosure vs. Short Sale: What Are My Pros And Cons?

Some financially distressed homeowners may end up finding a way that they can keep their home. However, for many, the circumstances that have caused their financial distress are not going to change any time soon: dropping home values, the sluggish economy, reduced income. For many, their only realistic and permanent way out is to get rid of the home and try to get a new start. Their options are either to negotiate a short sale, or to wait for their lender to foreclose. Here are some of the pros and cons of each option:

Taking Action

There is something to be said about taking action, rather than sitting around and having things happen to you. Being in financial distress is no fun for anyone. But working to solve your financial problems through a short sale at least means that you are taking charge, and you are making decisions: proactively working to make the best out of a bad situation. Foreclosure, on the other hand, is a waiting game. The lender calls the shots and decides the timing.

Closing The Books On A Bad Investment

By the time you find yourself making the decision on whether to pursue a short sale or to await foreclosure, it is clear that, for whatever the reason, you've realized that your home has turned out to be a bad investment. And the faster that you can close the books on a bad investment, the more quickly that you'll be able to allocate your resources to better income-generating opportunities. Provided that you get good advice and work with qualified short sale specialists, a short sale can often be completed in two to three months - whereas foreclosure make take a year or even longer.

Once you get yourself out of that losing position, you will sleep better at night, and you can focus on your future: using your skills to focus on income-producing activities, or perhaps upgrading your skills. You can put this bad investment in your past, and focus on the future. And the sooner you do that, the better.

Living Mortgage-Free And Rent-Free

One advantage of waiting for foreclosure is that, once you stop paying your mortgage, you are living mortgage-free and rent-free. There are some cases where homeowners have been able to continue living in their home for free for three years or more while the foreclosure process dragged on.

Some homeowners even actively prolong the foreclosure process, by applying for loan modifications that they know they will never be approved for, or by providing misleading or false information to their lender on loan-modification or short sale applications. They may justify these actions because they believe that the banks have taken advantage of them, and they feel it is a way to get their revenge. However, many of these foreclosure tactics are not ethical and many are not even legal.

There is a great deal of uncertainty associated with living in a home as you await foreclosure. In particular, if you have children, you are subjecting them to living in an unstable situation. You are living in an environment where creditors are contacting you my mail and by phone; you may stop opening your mail, and feel uncomfortable answering your phone. Even if you are not deliberately out there trying to game the system, most people do not feel good about themselves knowing that they are in default of an obligation and avoiding dealing with it.

Deficiency Judgments

The deficiency is the shortfall when repaying a mortgage after a foreclosure or a short sale. For example, if the proceeds going to the lender after selling a home come to $150,000, but there was $225,000 owing on the mortgage, the deficiency is $75,000. If the lender waives that deficiency, the borrower does not ever have to repay it. However, if the lender gets a deficiency judgment, you might be required to repay that deficiency at some point in the future.

How deficiency judgments work varies from state to state. (See Section 5.5: Recourse/non-recourse loans, and what this means for deficiency).

In a non-recourse state, if a lender forecloses on you, your property will be seized and sold to pay off the loan. But if the sale of the property does not generate enough to pay the total balance owing on your mortgage, they may not try to recover that deficiency balance from you. Once they have foreclosed upon you, you are not responsible to pay back that mortgage shortfall. In a recourse, state, however, a lender may sue you to recover the deficiency balance owing, or they may sell that deficiency to a debt collector. Some states also prohibit a lender from collecting a deficiency balance if the loan was used as purchase money.

In a short sale, whether the deficiency is waived or not depends both on the state and on the lender. Although only a few years ago it was difficult to get many lenders to agree in writing to waive the deficiency after a short sale, these days that has completely turned around.

Government short sale programs such as HAFA and FHA require lenders to waive the deficiency. And as of 2012, FHFA official guidelines (which apply to all loans where Freddie Mac or

Fannie Mae are the investors) are that, if a borrower has acted in good faith, the lender agrees that it will not pursue the deficiency. Since Freddie and Fannie are the investors in the majority of American home loans, this means that in the majority of short sales these days, the lenders do waive the right to pursue the deficiency. You can check whether your loan is owned by Freddie Mac by visiting https://ww3.freddiemac.com/corporate/, and check Fannie Mae by visiting https://www.knowyouroptions.com/loanlookup.

Credit Score And Credit Report

The credit-reporting agencies (the main ones are Experian, Equifax, and TransUnion) are notoriously tight-lipped about how they calculate credit scores, so it can be difficult to figure out what the hit to a credit score from a short sale is compared to from a foreclosure. Although some sources claim that a short sale affects credit score the same as a foreclosure, this does not appear to be true.

This misconception seems to come, at least partly, from the assumption that homeowners must default on their mortgage payments before attempting a short sale - which, as we have already seen, is no longer the case. In the past, homeowners had to be already delinquent before requesting a short sale. Delinquency hits credit scores hard. But now, homeowners may request a short sale from their lender before they are delinquent, or before their delinquency has been reported to credit-reporting agencies.

Many comments posted in online forums by people who have actually undertaken short sales show that the impact of a short sale is far less than that of foreclosure. For example:

June 28, 2010, comment on Loansafe web forum:

"I closed on the short sale on my home on April 19, 2010 (Citi and Freddie 30 yr fixed rate loan).

My credit reports have now reported the short sale as "settled for less than amount owed.

My Equifax score is now around 657. It was about 715 or so prior to the reporting of the short sale.

My Transunion score is now 637. It was 703 prior to the short sale.

I haven't checked Experian yet."

April 30, 2012, comment on Loansafe web forum:

"we completed a short sale two years ago while current. Bank even returned a payment that was electronically drafted the day after approval. Between the wife and I, we had about $80k in credit limits on cards. No limits or interest changed. In fact, last year two limits were raised because we quit using the cards. FICO scores dropped about 20 points right after but back up within 6 months."

June 28, 2012, comment on Loansafe web forum:

"In early May we closed on out HAFA Short Sale with BOA. Prior to becoming late on payments in October 2011 my score was in the 760s. So after completing the HAFA Short Sale my credit score dropped to 687. I was surprised! Thought it would be alot (sic) lower.

Reporting as closed

Payment Status: Legally paid in full for less than the full balance

No regrets and only wish I would have made the decision earlier."

For a borrower who has remained current on mortgage payments, the "hit" of a short sale on their record can be as little as 60 points or less, and it may remain on record for as little as 12 to 18 months. For borrowers who were behind on mortgage payments when they did the short sale, the hit may be more like 100 points or more. In contrast, a foreclosure may cost the borrower between 250 and 300 points. A foreclosure remains on the borrower's record for seven years. There is no set amount of points that a person loses for either action; rather, the higher your credit rating was to begin with, the more points you lose.

Since short sales are negotiated between borrowers and their lenders, most are reported to credit bureaus as "account paid in full with less than full balance" or "legally settled for less than owed." While a remark like this may have negative connotations, most future lenders will not perceive it to be as detrimental as a foreclosure on your record, because it shows that you communicated with your lender in an effort to proactively resolve the situation.

If your credit rating is important to you, this is an important reason to choose a short sale over foreclosure - and, if possible, to remain current on your mortgage payments throughout the short sale process. Maintaining your credit rating is especially important for any borrower who hopes to obtain any financing in the future (home loans, car loans, or competitive interest rates on credit cards).

Purchasing A Home In The Future

For homeowners who are trying to get rid of a home that is only losing them money, purchasing a new home may be the last thing on their mind. But once they have got rid of that old home, and got back on track with their finances, entering into the housing market again might seem more attractive. So it is important not to close off options for the future with the choices you make today.

If you have remained current on your mortgage payments throughout the short sale process, you may be able to qualify for a new home loan immediately following the short sale. If you were behind on mortgage payments when you did the short sale, you will probably have to wait two to three years before a new lender will give you financing.

If, on the other hand, your lender has foreclosed upon you, you will have to wait between five and seven years before a lender will consider giving you a loan. If there are "extenuating circumstances" leading to the foreclosure, e.g. death of a wage-earner, or illness or an accident resulting in injury, that waiting time might be dropped to three years.

The Stigma Of Foreclosure

Foreclosure is not for everyone. There are definitely people out there who feel it is their due to get revenge on the banks, and who stop paying their mortgages to see how long they can live rent-free for. But for most people, the uncertainty of wondering when the lender might foreclose, and when they will have to move, is not worth the stress that it causes.

And for many, there is the stigma of foreclosure. Your neighbors see the notices stapled to your door. Your friends and family know that you are being foreclosed upon. You, yourself, are going to bed each night knowing that you are defaulting on an obligation that you promised to pay.

Foreclosure may buy you some months, or even a year or more, of living rent-free. But you need to be able to live with yourself during the process - and also to feel good about yourself, and the choices you have made, afterward, too.

Chapter 5

What Factors Make A Lender Likely To Approve My Short Sale?

The most fundamental reason that a lender will approve a short sale is their bottom line: doing the math, and working out how to cut their losses. That said, though, there are many other factors that also influence a lender's decision on whether or not to approve a particular short sale, some of which you do have control of, listed below.

The Bottom Line

Some people might wonder why a lender would accept a payoff that is short of the full balance owing by approving a short sale. The answer is simple. It comes down to the bottom line: which recovery method will net them more.

If a borrower cannot continue to make payments, and the lender and the borrower do not make some sort of deal, the property will eventually go into foreclosure. This is a very expensive option for the lender: it is a lengthy process (which costs them money rather than earning money on their investment); they incur legal fees along the way; and they eventually are stuck with a devalued property, possibly in need of repairs, that they didn't want in the first place.

Lenders want to avoid this. If they can find a shorter and faster solution, which nets them the same or more in the end, they will overlook other issues such as demonstration of hardship, and pursue that. (The one exception to this may be some FHA-insured loans, as FHA tends to have a stricter qualifying process). In some cases, modifying the terms of the loan so that the loan becomes more affordable may be an appropriate solution - although both lenders and borrowers have found out that many loan modifications soon fail. Borrowers re-default, and then both parties have to go through the whole process again.

That is why lenders are increasingly veering towards short sales. They do take a loss on a short sale, but it is a smaller loss than what they would eventually take through foreclosure. And, unlike a loan modification, the solution is permanent: the mortgage is paid out and closed, and the devalued home is now owned by a third party. The borrower and lender are done with one another.

Does The Offer Represent FMV?

One of the first things that a lender will look at in a short sale application is whether the purchase offer (sales price) reflects Fair Market Value (FMV). This is because the lender, if they approve the short sale, is agreeing to take a loss on the money they loaned. They will consider taking that loss - but they will not want to take any more of a loss than is necessary. A lender will normally commission a Broker's Price Opinion (BPO) to determine what is FMV for the property at that time. (See Section 10.3: How does the bank put a price on the property?, below).

Demonstration Of Hardship

Most lenders, and most government short sale programs (see Chapter 16), have official guidelines requiring that the borrower has undergone some sort of hardship, which has led to their current state of financial distress. That said, as explained above, in most cases a lender's prime reason for approving a short sale is their bottom line. If they calculate that foreclosing will cost them more in the end, they will likely approve the short sale and overlook the hardship issue. (For more on the issue of hardship, and writing a hardship letter, see Section 12.8: How do I write a convincing hardship letter?).

Junior Lenders

Having junior lenders, or other lien-holders, can mean a few extra steps to the short sale approval process, but it doesn't necessarily represent a stumbling block to getting approval. Of course it is simpler if there is only one lien-holder, because then all document submissions and approvals deal with only that one lender.

However, if a property goes into foreclosure, junior lien-holders normally get nothing (other than the right to continue to pursue the borrower for a deficiency balance, which they may or may not ever succeed at collecting). This means that they are usually quite open to approving a short sale, because it at least gives them some opportunity to negotiate a small settlement. For them, anything is better than nothing. So they usually have no reason to hold up the process. (See Chapter 8: Dealing with junior mortgages or other liens, below).

Is There Mortgage Insurance?

In the past, having mortgage insurance (MI) on a loan put one more step in the whole process of gaining approval for a short sale. All loans where the buyer put less than 20% down payment require MI. But, in some cases, even when the borrower puts down more than 20%, the lender purchases MI without telling the borrower! So it is possible for a homeowner who is seeking approval for a short sale to be surprised to find out that they have a MI policy that they never knew about.

Although MI still may cause delays, and in some cases the mortgage insurer might not approve a short sale, recent changes to FHFA short sale guidelines mean that MI will no longer be the stumbling block it once was. In November 2012, Freddie Mac implemented changes to the short sale approval process that authorizes loan servicers to approve many short sales themselves - without even having to present the case to either the investor or the mortgage insurer.

For more about mortgage insurance, see Chapter 9: Mortgage insurance, below.

Meeting Deadlines

This is a part of the short sale approval process that is almost entirely in the hands of the borrower: meeting deadlines for submitting paperwork and providing information.

As part of the short sale process, your lender will send on-going requests for information. They need this information from you to evaluate your case and issue you an approval. Getting approval for a short sale can be a lengthy process, but it is also very time-sensitive. Frustrated buyers may only wait so long for a sale to close before walking away from a deal. And then you, the seller, have to start all over again: listing the home, and reassembling and resubmitting the short sale package to the lender.

Also, in many cases, the lender will have a trustee sale scheduled: if the short sale is not approved by a certain date, the auction will go ahead. (And remember, you cannot safely assume that your lender's foreclosure department and their short sale department are communicating with one another. There have been cases where a lender is on the edge of approving a short sale, but they go ahead with the trustee sale anyway).

So anything you can do to speed up the whole approval process increases the chance of your lender approving the short sale. This means responding promptly to any requests for information or documentation, and providing for on-going new information requests, such as monthly pay stubs, on time.

Dealing With Banks vs. Credit Unions

Credit unions are likely to approve a short sale. However, they are less likely to waive the deficiency balance on the loan or, if they do, they may require a cash contribution on closing and/or a promissory note signed by the seller, promising to repay either the full balance or a reduced balance.

The credit unions' justification for playing more "hard-core" with deficiency balances is that they must protect their members' or shareholders' investment.

However, even credit unions are loosening up on those requirements. If you are having trouble getting a credit union to agree to waive the deficiency balance, you still do have some negotiating power. It is worth attempting some polite conversations with your lender about how the options you have may affect their bottom line.

For example, if you refuse to go through with the short sale because the lender won't waive the deficiency balance, they will be forced to go through with foreclosure (if they are first lien-holder) which probably will result in a greater loss to them than the short sale will. And if they are a junior lien-holder, they will likely get nothing when the first forecloses. Although junior lien-holders may retain the right to pursue the borrower for the balance owing on the loan, lenders know that, in most cases, they will have little luck in collecting from a borrower who was financially strapped enough that they were foreclosed upon.

You also have the option of going through with the short sale, and then declaring bankruptcy afterward, which will eliminate your obligation to repay the deficiency balance anyway - and you most certainly can remind them of that.

Political Pressure

Yes, there is even political pressure on lenders to approve more short sales. This is because of settlements between the federal government and the large banks as a result of the banks' unlawful foreclosure practices (issues such as "robo-signing" of documents, incomplete document trails and lost documents, and missing documentation of who actually owns the loans). Part of that settlement agreement included a push from the government for lenders to stem foreclosures by approving more short sales.

Chapter 6

How Do I Deal With A Junior Mortgage Or Other Liens?

Can I Do A Short Sale If There Is More Than One Mortgage?

Yes! You can definitely do a short sale even if there are multiple mortgages on your home.

With so many homes underwater these days, junior lien-holders are unlikely to receive anything if the property is foreclosed upon. This means that junior lien-holders themselves are unlikely to exercise their right to foreclose. It also means that, if the first lender forecloses, junior lenders are usually open to making a deal: accepting a small payment to release their lien in order to allow the sale to go ahead. They know that if they refuse, and the first forecloses, they will get nothing.

However, the recourse that junior lien-holders have against the borrower/debtor is the deficiency judgment. Even just a few years ago, most junior lien-holders held on to their right to pursue borrowers for the deficiency balance on the loan. (Whether they, or the debt collectors they sold the deficiency rights to, would ever exercise that right, is another story - in many cases, that deficiency is simply filed as an uncollectable debt).

However, as the short sale industry matured, homeowners who used experienced negotiators to advocate for them came to realize that a short sale that does not relieve them of that deficiency balance obligation is not always a great deal. Homeowners became less willing to sign off on a short sale that includes a deficiency obligation. The juniors' requirements were stymying the whole process.

However, today, most short sale programs (e.g. HAFA, FHA, or loans sold to GSE's as stated in 2012 FHFA guidelines) waive the right of the lender to pursue the deficiency balance on the loan. Those categories cover the majority of American home mortgages. If a short sale is handled by experienced negotiators working on behalf of the seller, these days there are very few cases where a junior lender's approval letter does <u>not</u> waive the deficiency balance - usually in return for just the amount that the first lender is allowing them, and only occasionally requesting an additional payment from the seller.

What If There Are Other Liens On The Property?

Other liens on the property, such as HOA liens or judgment liens, work much the same way as junior mortgage liens. The liens get paid out in the order that they were recorded, regardless of the reason for the lien or the amount owing on it. The exception is tax liens, and some HOA liens, which may gain a higher priority than other liens, regardless of when the lien was put in place.

How Do I Approach The Junior Lien-Holders?

The first lien-holder will not likely approve a short sale unless they know that other lien-holders will release their liens too. So the best time to approach junior lien-holders is the same time that you submit the short sale package to the first lender (who is usually the foreclosing lender).

For second or third mortgage-holders, prepare and submit a complete short sale package, according to that lender's specific requirements, just as you would for your first mortgage-holder.

For other lien-holders, such as your Homeowner's Association or other creditors, write a courteous letter explaining the situation and requesting a lien release. HOA's may be more difficult to deal with that other lien-holders; they may be reluctant to negotiate. They may demand all back dues, while the foreclosing lien-holder may offer them only six or twelve months of back dues. However, HOA's generally do know that, if they don't release the lien and force your mortgage lender to foreclose, they will get little or nothing. So they will likely be prepared to talk.

You can attempt to negotiate the settlement amount with your HOA - remembering that your first mortgage lender will likely contribute something towards this settlement. Your best bet is to try to negotiate with both them and your lender - for example, offering the HOA six months of dues, and requesting your lender to pay the full balance owing - and hope that they will meet somewhere in the middle. If your short sale is being processed through HAFA or according to FHFA guidelines, an amount totaling between $6,000 and $8,500 will be available to help settle junior liens. You should be prepared to contribute some cash, too, if it helps to achieve that compromise. Normally, a HOA will require some cash settlement, which could range from a token $100 to full payment of the amount due.

If the junior lien-holders are holding out for more cash than you can offer, they may require you to sign an unsecured promissory note to be paid over a certain amount of time, e.g. a $10,000 note at zero interest, to be paid in monthly installments of $83.33 over a period of ten years. In some cases it may be in your best interest to sign the note in order to make the deal go ahead, even though it seems like a lot of money. But in other cases, the promissory may represent an obligation that you will not be able to afford. (Unlike a secured debt such as a mortgage or creditor's lien, a promissory note that is unsecured can be removed through bankruptcy). You should seek advice from an attorney and/or accounting professional before signing a promissory note, to determine whether it is in your interests to sign it, and whether declaring bankruptcy may be an appropriate move for you.

Chapter 7

What Is Mortgage Insurance?

Mortgage insurance (MI) has been a stumbling block to short sale approvals in the past. Fortunately, recent changes in FHFA short sale approval guidelines mean that many short sales will now have automatic MI approval.

How Mortgage Insurance Works

There are two types of mortgage insurance: borrower-paid private mortgage insurance, and lender-paid private mortgage insurance.

Borrower-paid private mortgage insurance is the type of mortgage insurance that most homeowners know about. It is also known as "traditional mortgage insurance," and it is required on any mortgage loans where the purchaser puts down less than a 20% down payment on the home. There is also private mortgage insurance that is lender-paid. It is sometimes thought of as a "hidden" mortgage insurance, because the borrower may not be aware of its existence. If a lender considers a borrower to be risky, they may choose to purchase mortgage insurance on a loan. Although the lender is the one purchasing the mortgage insurance, the borrower still ultimately pays for it because the premium will be built into the interest rate offered.

While mortgage insurance may seem like an unfair cost to borrowers who do not have a lot of cash on hand, what this mortgage insurance does is it actually allows higher-risk borrowers, who may not have otherwise been approved for a loan without that insurance, to get a loan.

Mortgage insurance is purchased for the benefit of the lender. It does not protect the borrower. Contrary to what many people believe, mortgage insurance does not cover the full value of a loan. Rather, the lender purchases a level of insurance coverage that represents a percentage of the amount loaned; the riskier the borrower is deemed to be, the higher rate of coverage they will purchase.

Mortgage Insurance And Short Sales

The good news about mortgage insurance is that changes to FHFA short sale approval guidelines, which took effect in November 2012, mean that many short sale applications will no longer have to go to the mortgage insurer for approval. Provided that the borrower meets some common basic guidelines (is either more than 30 days delinquent on their mortgage, or has suffered an eligible hardship such as divorce, permanent disability, or relocation for employment), loan servicers may bypass both the mortgage insurer and the investor, and authorize short sale approvals themselves. These FHFA guidelines apply to Freddie and Fannie loans - in other words, to the majority of mortgage loans.

However, for mortgage loans with mortgage insurance, and where either the borrower does not meet those guidelines, or from a lender who is using different guidelines (a non-Freddie, non-Fannie loan), the short sale will probably require approval from the mortgage insurer. The level of insurance coverage will influence what the minimum acceptable proceeds a lender will accept on a sale will be. For example, if the loan amount is for $100,000, and the lender has purchased 25% coverage, the maximum that the mortgage insurer will pay is $25,000. The lender will take the amount that the mortgage insurer will pay into account when determining the minimum proceeds that they will accept through the short sale.

If you are considering a short sale, it is important to determine whether or not there is private mortgage insurance on your loan, who the coverage is with, and what the coverage ratio is. It is important to be aware that private mortgage insurance follows the loan, even if the loan is sold, and that your loan investor may negotiate directly with your mortgage insurer.

Chapter 8

Short Sale FAQs

The information above presents all of the options available to financially distressed homeowners, as well as specific information about short sales and how and why lenders approve short sales. If you are considering a short sale, you will probably still have some questions about the whole process. This section goes through some of the frequently asked questions that homeowners have when they are considering a short sale.

Must I Already Be Delinquent?

Formerly, lenders required that homeowners be delinquent on their mortgage payments before the lender would even look at a short sale request. Today, however, most lenders will consider a short sale for a borrower who is at "imminent risk of default." This means that, even though you have not defaulted on mortgage payments yet, your cash flow is such that you soon will not be able to afford your mortgage payments - for example, if you have reduced income, or increased expenses, or if your mortgage is about to reset to a new, higher monthly rate that you will not be able to afford.

Lenders want to make a profit. Failing that, they at least want to make their losses as small as possible. If they see that your loan will soon be costing them money, most lenders these days will work with you on finding a solution - even before you become delinquent.

Some government short sale programs have specific guidelines regarding default:

- FHA: the borrower must be in default, or current but facing imminent default, in order to apply; borrower must be at least 31 days delinquent by the time the short sale closes.

- VA: no default requirement, but borrower must demonstrate hardship.

- HAFA: the loan must either be in default, or default is reasonably foreseeable.

- FHFA (applies to Freddie Mac and Fannie Mae loans): the homeowner is more than 30 days delinquent or has undergone an eligible hardship.

Must I Already Have An Offer On The Home?

This is another part of the short sale process that has changed in recent years. Formerly, you needed to present an offer to your lender in order to request a short sale approval. But today, many lenders will pre-approve a short sale while you are marketing the property.

A few years ago, many short sale deals fell through because they took so long. You could not start the process until you had a buyer. Often, by the time the lender was close to approving the deal, the buyer had become frustrated and walked. If the buyer did stick around, deals sometimes fell through because the offered price turned out to be nowhere near what the lender required.

If you can get your lender to pre-approve a short sale, you speed up the process. But, more importantly, you know in advance what your lender's minimum net proceeds requirement is - so you know when not to waste your time with a buyer whose purchase offer is too low.

Some short sale programs will automatically pre-approve a short sale. For example, the FHA Pre-foreclosure Sale program requires that borrowers meet the basic eligibility requirements and apply for a short sale before they even list the home. (In reality, though, many brokers will list a home and obtain a purchase offer before going through the application process). Likewise, the HAFA program allows for pre-approval of a short sale, before the home is listed. And some of the bank's own short sale programs, for example the Bank of America Cooperative Sale Program are pro-active in that the lender contacts the seller - in effect, pre-approving them when they request that they do a short sale.

How Does The Bank Put A Price On The Property?

The lender will commission a Broker's Price Opinion (BPO), which is a real estate broker's estimate of the value of the home, taking into account the condition of the home, recent sales in the neighborhood, and current market conditions. The lender will usually expect to see a sales price that is around or above that BPO.

If a purchase offer is received that is below the lender's BPO, the lender may not approve the short sale. A homeowner (or, better, their short sale negotiator) can challenge a lender's BPO if they think it is too high. For more about challenging a BPO, see Section 12.4: About the BPO, below.

Who Pays Expenses Associated With The Sale?

Short sales are different from regular real estate transactions in that the seller is not expected to pay any of the commissions or closing costs. This is because all of the parties involved in the short sale know that the seller does not have any cash to spare: that is why they are doing the short sale. Commissions and closing costs are normally paid by the lender, by being deducted from the proceeds they receive following the sale. Occasionally, some closing costs may also be paid by the buyer. The only costs a seller might have to pay would be if one of their lenders requires that they make a cash contribution on closing, or requires them to sign a promissory note. Most short sales these days do not require contributions from the seller; if there is a seller's contribution required, it will be spelled out in the lender's short sale approval letter.

How Long Can I Expect The Process To Take?

A short sale cannot proceed without having a buyer - so part of the timeline for completing a short sale depends upon putting a realistic sales price on the property, and marketing it properly.

A few years ago, short sales took many months or even a year or more to make their way through the approval process. This is because lenders were flooded with requests, and did not have enough personnel to deal with them. Back then, many real estate agents were not yet experienced in dealing with short sales either, so they made many mistakes and omissions in the documentation they submitted. However, today, short sales are proceeding much more quickly. The majority of short sales, whether pre-approved or not, take 60 to 90 days. Occasionally they go through in less than a month.

If the short sale has not been pre-approved, the whole approval process may take between a couple of weeks and a couple of months, once a buyer has been found and the completed short sale package has been submitted to the lender. Having an experienced short sale negotiator working for you at this stage will speed up the process substantially, as a good negotiator will prevent avoidable delays caused by incorrect or missing paperwork. They will know how and when to follow up with your lender to keep your file at the top of their pile, and when to demand that they escalate your case.

Many of the government short sale programs now have guidelines to avoid delays in the approval process. Although these are only guidelines, not enforceable regulations, they are helping to streamline the short sale process. For example, FHFA guidelines now require that a lender acknowledge receipt of the purchase offer within three days, and that they either make a decision about the short sale request within 30 days, or they provide a reason for the delay and then provide the borrower with weekly progress updates. For a HAFA short sale, the lender must approve or deny the short

sale with 10 days of receiving a purchase offer and completed
Request for Approval of Short Sale form.

Can A Friend Or Relative Buy The Home From Me?

In most cases, as a condition of the short sale approval, the lender
will require that you sign a form confirming that this is an "arm's
length transaction" - affirming that the buyer and seller are
"unrelated and unaffiliated by family, marriage, or commercial
enterprise" (or wording along that line). They may also make this a
requirement between other parties to the short sale, such as buyer's
agent, seller's agent, and third-party short sale negotiators.

The reason for this is requirement is to prevent fraud. The
lender is taking a loss by approving a short sale, and they want to
know that the seller is negotiating in good faith: that they really are
in financial distress; that the selling price represents fair market
value; and that there are no deals going on behind their back that
someone else is going to profit from. They agree to take that loss on
the condition that the seller is not going to benefit from the short
sale. If a relative or friend is going to purchase the home at the
reduced short sale price, and then rent it to you or sell it back to you,
the banks will see that as you benefiting from the sale.

However, it is possible that a friend or relative legitimately
wants to buy your house. In that case, make sure that you disclose
the relationship that you have with the buyer to the lender. If the
offer is legitimate and represents fair market value, and your lender
deems it is in their best interest to accept that offer, they may not
hold you to the arm's length requirement.

If I Have Money In Savings, Will They Take That Away From Me If They Approve The Deal?

Your mortgage lender will want full access to your financial
information. In order to approve a short sale, they need evidence that

you are not able to pay your mortgage. If you have substantial savings tucked away, your lender may conclude that you do actually have the means to make your mortgage payments, and they may deny approval for the short sale. Or they may require that you make a cash contribution in order to offset some of their losses.

If your lender reviews your last 60 days of bank statements and sees that you have over $10,000 in savings, they will likely ask you for a cash contribution in order to approve the short sale. If your loan is with the same bank as your savings accounts, it is possible that your lender will pull money from those accounts - even if they have never done an auto-payment from them in the past.

Remember, the idea of a short sale is for both parties - the homeowner and the mortgage lender - to get out of a losing situation. Both parties are going to lose some money out of the deal. If the lender sees that you have money in the bank, they will not want to take the full loss themselves. They probably (and reasonably) will expect that you contribute something to share a fair part of the loss.

Is My Income Too High For The Lender To Approve My Short Sale?

The short answer is that there are no set maximum income limits for a lender to approve a short sale. Rather, the lender looks at cash flow: your income relative to your expenses, which affects your ability to pay. Some government short sale programs do have some guidelines regarding income. For example, the FHA Pre-foreclosure Sale Program requires that the borrower's inability to pay is a result of a change in their financial situation: either a drop in income, or increased living expenses.

The original qualification requirements for HAFA had no actual income limit, but they did have a requirement regarding mortgage payments relative to income: the mortgage payments had to be more than 31% of gross monthly income to qualify. However, since February 2011, that requirement has been dropped.

It is advisable to check with your own lender early in the application process, though, as some servicers may implement their own maximum income requirements.

If I Stop Paying My Mortgage, So The Total Debt I Owe Gets Even Bigger, Won't My Lender Be Less Likely To Approve The Sale?

Not necessarily. Remember, the lender's decision comes down to the bottom line. It's not about the dollar value of how much you owe, it is about how they can minimize their losses. From the lender's point of view, more important than the actual loan balance are:

- Does the purchase offer represent fair market value? The lender will take a loss, but they need to know it is a reasonable loss. They don't want to see some buyer get an unfairly good deal while they themselves take a loss.

- What recovery method will net them more in the end: a short sale now, or a foreclosure and REO (bank-owned property) sale some time down the road?

Can I Expect To See Any Money Out Of This?

You cannot expect to see any money from the actual short sale itself. In a short sale, the sales proceeds are "short" of the balance owing to the lender and other lien-holder(s), so all of the proceeds go towards those debts.

However, there are numerous incentive programs that provide cash to homeowners who complete a short sale (See Chapter 16: Short sale programs and incentives, below). Usually this cash incentive is labeled as a contribution towards relocation expenses, and is payable to the seller by the lender after the sale closes. Cash incentives range from $750 or $1,000 for completing an FHA short sale, to $3,000 for completing a HAFA or FHFA short sale, to up to $35,000 through some lenders' own short sale programs.

Can I Get My Home Back After A Short Sale?

A short sale, like any real estate sale, is a binding contract. Title to the home goes to the new purchaser.

Some homeowners may be enticed by agreements where a buyer purchases their home with some agreement to either rent the home back to the original owner, or to purchase it back at a later date. Most of these proposals are actually either scams or are fraudulent transactions. Some scams work by agreements where, if the seller meets certain conditions, they have the right to purchase the home back after a few years - but the scammer knows that the seller has almost no chance of being able to meet those conditions, and ends up getting to keep the home they purchased at a bargain price. (See Chapter 20: Scams to watch out for, below).

Deals where the seller has the right to rent the home or purchase the home back are usually not permitted by the lender; they do not usually fit the lender's requirement of the sale being an "arm's-length transaction." If you are considering a deal like this, make sure you disclose it to your lender, or you could find yourself facing charges of fraud.

In some states, after foreclosure there is a set time period (usually between six months and a year) that the homeowner has the possibility of paying out the mortgage and getting their home back. This is known as Owner's Right of Redemption - but it applies only to foreclosure, and not to a short sale.

Chapter 9

What Decisions Do I Need To Make During This Process?

If you have reviewed all of your options, and concluded that a short sale is the best option for your situation, you will need to make some decisions about exactly how to proceed. While it may seem stressful to have to make these decisions, it is important to also remember that it is also empowering to be making your own decisions, compared to the feelings of helplessness and hopelessness that the foreclosure process brings. Take charge, do your research, and make wise and informed choices.

Do I Need A Real Estate Agent?

It is highly recommended to work with a real estate agent when conducting a short sale. Even for any real estate sale - a selling agent (or listing agent) works on your behalf to look out for your interests, and to protect you by advising you about your legal obligations and the legal implications of any document or contract you sign. A selling agent also is able to present your property to the maximum number of buyers.

Many home sellers find the idea of selling their home without an agent attractive. After all, an agent earns a commission of 5 to 6% of the sales price, and there are now numerous For-Sale-by-Owner websites out there. If they can sell their home without an agent, they can save thousands of dollars.

This may make sense for some people in a traditional real estate sale. However, in the case of a short sale, the agents' commission is part of the closing costs of the sale. It is deducted from the net proceeds of the sale - which means the lender pays the commission, not the seller.

For that reason alone, it makes sense to work with a real estate agent - in particular, an agent who is experienced in short sales - who will market your home, and advise you and look out for your interests. Because those services are all at your lender's expense.

What About Third-Party Short Sale Negotiators?

Short sales are complex transactions. They require a specialist's knowledge and experience: all of the ins and outs of a system with guidelines that seem to be changing every few months. In addition, each lender works differently. They have different requirements for their short sale submission packages. Some are more or less likely to approve a short sale. Some are more or less likely to waive their right to collect the deficiency balance.

There are many real estate agents who are reluctant to take on a home sale that is a short sale. This is because they have tried a few short sales, and few or none worked out. The lender demanded different paperwork than what they submitted, the process dragged on, and eventually the whole thing fell apart: either the buyer finally walked, or the trustee sale date came up and time ran out.

This is where short sale specialists can help. There are real estate agents who specialize in short sales. There are also companies that specialize in negotiating short sales, and that work by having a network of all of the professionals you need (whether in-house or as affiliates) to make your short sale application go through: from real estate agents to attorneys to tax accountants.

Typically, a short sale negotiating company will work by assigning you a specific person to work as your negotiator, so you have one person you can contact and who is familiar with your case.

If you are working through a law firm, your negotiator may be a paralegal. Your negotiator coordinates the work of the other professionals working on your file, and also handles all of the contact and negotiations with your lender(s). Your negotiator advocates for you: they seek to expedite the whole short sale negotiation process; they assemble and provide all required financial documentation to the lender(s); they work to release all of the liens so the sale can proceed; and they work towards negotiating the very best deal they can for you. (Although you may not be seeing any cash from the actual sales proceeds, successful negotiations usually include having you waived of having to repay any deficiency balances, and possibly negotiating some cash for your relocation costs).

The advantage of using specialist short sale negotiators is that they are working on short sales every day. While most homeowners contemplating a short sale will do only one short sale in their whole life, a good short sale negotiator will have coordinated hundreds of short sales transactions. They know how each lender works and what each lender requires; in many cases, they have handled enough cases that they even know the lender's negotiators personally.

How To Choose Short Sale Negotiator

Short sales are complex transactions, and time is of the essence. If paperwork is mishandled, or if deadlines are not met, a short sale may fall apart. When choosing the short sale specialist who is going to negotiate for you, do your homework: make sure that they are experienced, and have handled dozens, if not more, short sale transactions. Specifically, some things to check are:

- How many short sale approvals have they negotiated, and what is their success rate?

- Do they have some sort of documentation that you can check, to verify their short sales claims? You want to look for either a list of actual properties that have been sold, or actual short sale approval letters that they have obtained.

- Do they have references that you can contact, of homeowners who they have worked with, or client testimonials?

- Have they managed to obtain previous short sale approvals from your specific lender?

Remember that how your short sale request turns out will affect your life for years to come: whether the sale goes through or not; what gets recorded on your credit report; whether you are responsible to pay back any deficiency balances or not. And, in a short sale, you do not have a lot of time to negotiate all of this. Look for the most experienced short sale negotiator you can find, who has a strong and reliable track record of closing deals.

Should I Default On My Mortgage Payments?

For some people, defaulting on their mortgage payments is not a choice: there simply is not enough money to go around. If there is not enough cash to meet the monthly expenses, putting food on the family table usually wins out over paying the mortgage.

For others, though, there may be the option of finding money: by paying the mortgage with credit cards; or by eating away at retirement savings to make the monthly payments. In this case, a decision needs to be made.

If the financial hardship leading to the lack of cash is only temporary, for example if the homeowner is off work for only a few months due to a medical condition, then it may be worth putting mortgage payments on high-interest credit cards or digging into savings. But if there is no end in sight - for example, for a homeowner has been laid off and doesn't know when he will get back to work - then using credit cards or eating into savings only delays the inevitable. And causes more problems.

The ideal for any homeowner is to never default on mortgage payments. Short sales or foreclosure aside, delinquent mortgage payments put a heavy hit on your credit score - especially if you are several months delinquent. But if you have gone through the numbers, and realize that you will soon no longer be able to afford your mortgage payments, the best thing to do is to contact your lender to let them know about your situation. Most lenders will work with a borrower who they consider "at imminent risk of default," especially if there is an identifiable hardship (reduced income/increased expenses), and they generally look positively at borrowers who are proactively trying to find solutions.

However, some lenders simply will not look at an offer on a short sale if a homeowner is current on their mortgage. This leads some homeowners to deliberately default on their mortgage payments; see Section 3.4 Strategic default, above.

Should I Stay Current On My Property Tax?

There is no need to stay current on property tax, as property tax debt runs with the land, not with the debtor. Outstanding property tax will be settled by your lender when the sale closes, as part of the closing costs.

Should I Stay Current On My Homeowner's Insurance?

Yes, definitely stay current on your homeowner's insurance. If something happens to the house (such as flood or fire) while you are still on title, you may be held personally liable for the costs if your insurance coverage has lapsed.

Check whether your home insurance payments are paid through escrow (through your mortgage) or if you are paying them separately, outside of your mortgage. If they are paid through escrow, this means that your lender will continue to make the payments until the escrow funds are gone, after which they will have to pay forced insurance coverage. If you are making the payments yourself, make sure to keep making them.

Should I Stay Current On HOA Fees?

If you live in a property managed by a Homeowners Association (or Condominium Owners Association), always stay current on your fees. This is because if you owe money to your HOA, they will automatically put a lien on your property, which prevents the property from being sold until you have either paid the overdue fees or come to a settlement with them - all of which delay the short sale process. In addition, if you live in a state that grants "super-priority lien" status to HOA liens, your HOA might actually initiate the foreclosure process.

Chapter 10

What Are The Steps In The Short Sale Process?

The steps to initiate a short sale can be different in different cases, depending upon the lender you are working with, and depending upon whether or not you qualify for a government short sale program or for an in-house incentive program by your lender (see Chapter 16: Short sale programs and incentives). The first thing you need to do is see if you qualify for a short sale program or incentive program. This will then help you to decide what works best for you: listing the home for sale, and waiting until you get a purchase offer before submitting the short sale request to your lender; or requesting a pre-approved short sale from your lender before you list your home.

How the short sale process flows in your particular case also depends whether you attempt to go it alone, or whether you choose to work with a specialist short sales negotiator. An experienced specialist negotiator will know how different lenders work, and what their specific short sale package requirements are; if you work with a specialist, they will make sure that the various steps in the process are carried out in the right order and that deadlines set by your lender, or by the buyer or by any other parties, are met.

If you choose to go it alone, your first step should be contacting your lender, to try to find out what programs you are eligible for, whether they will consider pre-approving a short sale that does not yet have a buyer, and specifically what they need you to submit in your short sale package. Beware: contacting your lender and finding the right person to answer your questions may not be easy.

Most departments that handle short sales are quite overwhelmed these days. If you are a homeowner, be prepared to be spend lots of time on hold, and to being transferred from department to department, in your quest to get a real human who can help you. Different lenders have different names for the department that deals with short sales, such as "loss mitigation," "work-out," and, ironically, "home retention." Try to find the correct department that you want to deal with. If you do manage to get through to someone, try to get a direct phone number so you can call them, or at least their department, directly in the future.

If you are having a short sales specialist or real estate agent handle your short sale for you, you will need to sign a letter authorizing your lender to discuss your case and any personal details such as your finances with them. Without that letter, your lender will not discuss your confidential information, so make sure that you list every person or party (for example your attorney, your tax accountant) who may be contacting them on your behalf in it. You can name individual people in the letter, and you can also authorize all employees of a specific company, e.g. of your real estate agency. The authorization letter must include the full names and social security numbers of all the borrowers on the loan, the loan number, and the address of the property.

Since the short sale process will vary from case to case, depending upon which short sale programs you are eligible for and whether you are working with a short sales negotiator or on your own, the process will not proceed in exactly the same order for every homeowner. For example, some may submit the short sale package before listing the home, and others will do it the other way around. But these general steps will apply to every sale.

Who Are The Players Involved?

A short sale is a complex transaction. Representing you, there will be yourself (the seller), your real estate agent, and any other parties who are assisting you to negotiate the short sale, such as a specialist short sale negotiator, your attorney, your financial planner or your accountant. Then there will be the buyer, the buyer's real estate agent, and the lender that the buyer is seeking financing from (unless they do not require financing).

Then there is your lender. Your file will probably begin in the hands of a document processor. Once all of the documentation has been received, and is complete and up-to-date to the lender's satisfaction, the file is normally passed to the lender's negotiator for review. It is not uncommon for a case to be transferred through several negotiators before an approval decision is reached.

Other parties who may come into play in the approval process are the investor and the mortgage insurer. If your lender is only the servicer of the loan, but not the actual investor of the loan, the file may also have to be sent to the investor for approval. And if there is mortgage insurance, the mortgage insurer may also review the file. Fortunately, new FHFA guidelines which took effect in November 2012 mean that many short sale approvals are now issued by loan servicers, and investors and mortgage insurers no longer need to review and approve the file in many cases.

What Can I Expect From Them?

In order to know what to expect from the different parties, it is important to always remember who is working for you and looking out for your best interests, such as your real estate agent and your short sale negotiator, and any other parties such as your attorney or your accountant. You can expect the professionals who are working for you to provide you with the best advice for your unique financial situation.

Parties working for the other "sides" - for the buyer and for the lender - are also expected to behave as professionals. But it is important for you to remember that their obligation is to look out for their own client, and not for you: that's their job. Make sure you surround yourself with your own qualified professionals who will be giving you the very best advice possible.

What Will Be Expected Of Me?

You will be expected to be open and honest, and to provide accurate information in a timely matter. The amount of information you will be required to share, particularly the details about your finances, when conducting a short sale, may make you uncomfortable. But it is important to remember that your lender needs complete and accurate information in order to be able to approve your short sale.

Do not hide information. If there are problems with the home, disclose them. If you have money put away in a savings account, disclose that. If the buyer of your home is actually your great-aunt Mary, disclose it. If you are found later to have hidden information, you may be found guilty of fraud. If your lender later finds that you were not negotiating "in good faith" they may require you to repay a deficiency that would have been waived.

Provide all documentation as soon as requested. Short sales are complex transactions, and some deals end up falling apart because of too many delays: the buyer walks, or the trustee sale date comes up before the sale is approved. It is in your best interest that this sale goes through, so make sure that you are not the cause of any delays because you did not provide information or documents promptly.

About The BPO

Your own listing agent will do a comparative market analysis (CMA), which shows selling prices of similar homes in your neighborhood that have sold recently, as well as what other comparable homes are currently priced at. The CMA will be used to determine how to price your property. The listing agent will also normally prepare a Broker's Price Opinion (BPO), which takes into account the condition of the home, recent sales in the neighborhood, and current market conditions, and provide that to the lender and to the lender's BPO agent.

It is important that you let any appraiser or broker who is doing the evaluation of the property know everything that is wrong with the property. The lower the BPO comes out to, the easier it will be for you to find a purchase offer that meets the price suggested by the BPO.

Your lender will normally conduct their own internal BPO, too. This is so they can determine how much they would likely receive if they were to sell the home through foreclosure, and to compare that number with the purchase offer price. If a lender gets a BPO that is higher than the purchase offer you have received, they may conclude that they will recover more by foreclosing on the property. A high BPO may slow, or completely halt, the short sale process.

If you believe that your lender's BPO is unrealistically high, you should immediately contact them and demand that they get another BPO. The BPO is, after all, just one broker's opinion. They may have overlooked some of the home's defects, or they may not have had up-to-date information on recent comparable sales. Forward your own BPO to them, or request that they conduct another BPO. Some lenders are open to discussing the BPO and some aren't. But if you believe that their BPO is too high, you should do your best to get them to revise it.

In most cases, lenders are supposed to share their BPO with you and your agent - but sometimes it is hard to get them to do that. HUD guidelines for the FHA program state that lenders should share the BPO, but sometimes it may take numerous requests, and even threats, to get them to do so. The November 2012 FHFA guidelines that servicers share the BPO with the seller to provide listing guidance apply to Freddie and Fannie loans - which takes in the majority of, but not all, loans.

Picking A Price, And Listing The Home

You might negotiate a pre-approved short sale with your lender before listing, or you may want to first find a buyer before submitting your short sale request to your lender. But, either way, you are going to have to pick a sales price and list your home.

Your real estate agent will help you to pick an appropriate listing price. A good real estate agent will evaluate the home itself, and will also look at recent sales of comparable homes in your neighborhood, to come up with a price that reflects fair market value: the likely reasonable selling price of your home.

It may be tempting for you to put a low asking price on your home, since you are not going to receive anything from the sale anyway. However, the higher the sales price, the more likely your lender is to approve the short sale.

Your lender will expect any purchase offer to be around or above the value obtained in their BPO. This is because the short sale represents a loss to them; they want to at least make sure that the home was sold at a fair price, and that they recovered as much as possible from the mortgage loan. If you can get access to the lender's BPO, this will help when you receive a purchase offer. That way you won't waste your time by accepting a purchase offer that your lender will not likely approve.

FHFA guidelines, for any loans where Freddie Mac or Fannie Mae is the investor, state that the lender is to undertake a BPO "as early as possible" in the short sale process, and that they are to use that BPO to provide guidance in choosing a listing price to the borrower and their agent. There is no requirement that the home be listed at the price recommended by the lender (or, in fact, that an offer at the suggested price will be accepted by the lender) - but the recommended listing price based on the BPO gives a good idea of what the lender will or will not approve.

The Listing Agreement

In general, the listing agreement for a short sale is pretty similar to the listing agreement for any normal real estate sale. However, there are a few things specific to a short sale that you should pay attention to.

Some listing agreements will state that, if you take the house off the market for any reason, you will still owe the agent a fee. You should not agree to this in a short sale, because if you suddenly somehow come across some money, for example through an inheritance, you may decide to keep your home and want to pull it off the market. You don't want to be obligated to pay the agent a fee if this happens.

It is also important to specify that the agent's commission is payable only upon completion of the sale, and not simply for the agent producing a willing buyer. This is because a short sale is subject to the lender's approval. Even with a willing buyer, it is possible that the sale may not go ahead. You do not want to be obligated to pay a commission for a sale that did not go through.

What Goes In The Short Sale Package?

Every lender has somewhat different requirements for what should be contained in a short sale package. If you have a short sale specialist working for you, they will put together the short sale package for you. Your role is simply to provide the documentation that your specialist requests from you as quickly as possible, to keep the whole process moving forward as quickly as possible.

If you are putting the short sale package together yourself, contact your lender to find out exactly what they need from you. Use a checklist, and make sure that every document they require is complete. Delays or omissions in your short sale package only harm you: they make it less likely that your file will make it to approval.

While each lender's requirements are different, here is a sample of the documents that most lenders will want included:

- an authorization letter, for the parties working for you (e.g. your negotiator, your agent, your attorney) to speak on your behalf to your lender

- a hardship letter, outlining the circumstances (reduced income, increased expenses) that have led to your troubles in meeting your mortgage payments, as well as supporting documentation (e.g. disability statements, unemployment check stubs; medical bills)

- your Financial Statement, or an Income, Expense and Asset Worksheet (i.e. Profit and Loss statement if self-employed, or 710 Uniform Borrower Assistance Form from everyone else)

- supporting financial information, including: tax returns and W-2 or 1040 forms for the past two years; one month of pay stubs; last two months bank statements

- estimates for any repairs needed to the property (if available)

- your agent's BPO or completive market analysis

- payoff statements from other lien-holders

- a preliminary HUD-1 settlement sheet

- if you already have a purchase offer: written proof of the buyer's ability to purchase (e.g. a pre-approval letter from their mortgage lender); and a copy of the purchase offer, signed by the buyer.

How Do I Write A Convincing Hardship Letter?

A hardship letter is a polite letter addressed to your lender that explains the circumstances that have contributed to you no longer being able to make your mortgage payments, and requesting that your lender approve you for a short sale. While you probably feel emotional about the financial challenges you are facing, the tone of the letter should be reasonable, and not overly emotional.

Important parts of a hardship letter are:

- an explanation of the circumstances that have led to the hardship, and their timing (e.g. you were laid off from your job 15 months ago, or three years ago a family member was diagnosed with a medical condition)

- how you have tried to deal with the situation (e.g. attempting a loan-modification, trying to sell the house, paying the mortgage on credit cards or from retirement savings)

- acknowledgement that your attempts to deal with the situation have not worked: the only option to avoid foreclosure is to attempt a short sale

- a listing of any repairs that are required, such as a leaking roof or torn carpets, and that you do not have the funds to complete these repairs

- a polite request to your lender asking them to work with you by considering approving you for a short sale

- an explanation that you always intended to meet your mortgage payments and that you wanted to keep the home - but things have just not worked out

- a thank you to your lender for considering your request.

Make sure that all of the documentation supporting your hardship is included with the hardship letter.

Preparing Your Home To Show

It may feel hard to get motivated to prepare your home to show, when you are not going to receive the proceeds from the sale. But remember: this sale is in your best interest. It is your chance to salvage your credit by avoiding a foreclosure on your record, and to pay off the mortgage debt that you can no longer afford. The sooner the home sells, the sooner you can close the books on this bad investment, and turn your attention to moving forward, not looking back.

You don't want to attract a low offer because your home is in poor condition. Your lender is far less likely to approve the short sale if the offer is too low. A home that is in good shape and looks cared-for is more likely to attract an offer around market price.

Preparing your home to sell via a short sale is much the same as preparing a home for a traditional real estate sale. Clean it up, and undertake any necessary small repairs or minor painting jobs. Remove what you can from the home, so it doesn't appear cluttered, and keep countertops and tables clear. Put some time into the yard: keeping the lawn mowed, cleaning up garden beds, and trimming shrubbery.

The one difference, though, between a traditional real estate sale and a short sale is that you should not invest money into major repairs or renovations. While it might be worth a homeowner doing a traditional sale to sink a few thousand dollars into painting or replacing carpeting, because that investment will likely come back to them, it is not worth it for the seller in a short sale (who is already tight on cash!) to invest in home improvements. Those repairs will either come from the lender upon closing, or from the buyer.

Chapter 11

How Do I Negotiate And Close My Short Sale?

Who Actually Approves The Short Sale?

Your lender (specifically, your loan servicer: whoever you normally make your mortgage payments to, usually a bank or credit union) is the one who will issue you the short sale approval. The approval letter normally will come on your lender's letterhead. Occasionally, approval letters will be issued by your lender's attorney or by a debt collector working on their behalf.

While your lender will be the one who issues the approval letter, in some cases the short sale request must also pass approval by the investor (the actual owner of the loan) and/or by the mortgage insurer.

What If They Counter Rather Than Approve?

Your request for the short sale approval will include the offered purchase price, and an accounting of the closing costs (including commissions, and payoffs to any junior lien-holders). Subtracting the closing costs from the purchase price leaves the net proceeds available to pay the first lender. If those net proceeds do not meet the lender's acceptable minimum, the lender may counter the offer, requesting that the net proceeds be raised (usually by raising the purchase price).

Here is where you can benefit from having an experienced short sale negotiator working on your behalf. Asking the buyer to raise their offer is one way to meet the lender's minimum requirements. However, there is usually some conciliation that can be done from the lender's side too. For example, if the original purchase offer is for $200,000, but the lender says that that offer will not meet their minimum net proceeds and wants the offer raised to $225,000, there is a good chance that they can be convinced to meet in the middle: drop their minimum net slightly if the buyer agrees to come up to, for example, $210,000.

If the buyer absolutely will not raise the purchase price, then there are two possibilities.

If the lender's BPO is too high, they may be expecting an unrealistically high sales price (see Section 12.4: About the BPO, above). You may try to get them to reassess their BPO. However, if their BPO is fair, and the buyer is just trying to get a rock-bottom deal and refuses to budge, then your best bet is to relist the property, and find a more active buyer who is willing to pay the price the lender is asking for. Short sales are becoming increasingly popular, both with investors and with people looking to enter the housing market for the first time; there are lots of buyers out there.

What If They Say No?

If your lender rejects your short sale request first time around, don't give up. Often, a short sale will be approved the second, third, or even fourth time around.

Look at why they rejected the short sale. If the problem is that the offered price does not meet their minimum acceptable net proceeds, look at negotiating some middle ground between what the buyer will come up to and what they will come down to, as described above, or finding a new buyer.

One common reason for the lender to reject a short sale is that they deem that there is "no hardship." However, most struggling homeowners have something that got them to where they are now: some incident that caused their income to be reduced, or their expenses to be increased. Look at your own history, and what events led up to your financial problems. Then look at the hardship letter your wrote (perhaps reviewing the advice in Section 12.8: How do I write a convincing hardship letter? above) and see if you can rewrite your hardship letter to make your case more convincing.

Another reason is that the lender might go through the financial documents and determine that no short sale is necessary because you have the financial resources to pay your mortgage. In that case, review the documentation to see that you have included all of your expenses and debts. Sometimes submitting revised documentation will get the lender to reconsider the case. (Here, also, is where having an experienced short sale negotiator reviewing everything for you can be an advantage). Perhaps offering them a small cash contribution will convince them to review the case.

Sometimes, simply sitting on the file for a month or so before resubmitting it may make a difference. The case may be reviewed by a new person this time, and your result may just come out positive.

The Approval Letter

Once your lender approves the short sale, they will issue you with an approval letter. If you have two mortgages with one lender, they may send you two separate letters (possibly even issued by different negotiators in different departments), or they may treat your two loans together, and issue one approval letter for the package.

Approval letters vary from lender to lender; they can range from one paragraph, to many pages in length. There are numerous issues that should be covered in your approval letter - but not all approval letters are as complete as they should be. Issues that should be addressed are:

- Identifying information: Listing you and any other borrowers on the mortgage, the loan number, and the property address.

- Approval: Some wording that indicates that the lender is approving the short sale or the short payoff of the loan.

- Minimum net proceeds: The minimum amount that the lender will accept following the sale (sales price minus closing costs and commissions).

- Lien release: A statement that the lender will release the lien on the property once the conditions of the sale have been met.

- Deficiency wording: Some statement regarding the deficiency, indicating either that the lender is waiving the borrower of having to repay the deficiency balance, or that the lender reserves the right to pursue the deficiency balance. Sometimes the wording can be confusing, or even absent, but it is very important that your approval letter addresses the deficiency balance. If there is no wording at all about the deficiency, this means that the deficiency balance is not waived. For more information, see Chapter 14: Deficiency balance, below.

- Closing date: Usually between 30 and 45 days after the date on the approval letter. If the sale has not closed by this date, the lender may withdraw their approval for the short sale.

- Payment instructions: Where the sales proceeds must be sent (usually an account they are to be wired to), and by what date (usually the same as the closing date).

Approval letters may also contain a statement about how the short sale will be reported to the various credit-reporting agencies. The usual wording is "account settled in full for less than full balance." They also usually state something about the tax consequences of forgiven debt: either that the lender will issue you a 1099 form, or that the forgiven debt will be reported to the IRS.

Some short sale approval letters list other conditions to the sale. Common conditions are listing the buyers' names, indicating that the approval is only valid for those buyers, and itemizing the closing costs that the lender will (and will not) pay including the agents' commissions. Some approval letters also indicate that the approval is contingent on the borrower either making a cash payment to the lender or signing a promissory note.

It is always a good idea to have your attorney review you approval letter for you - especially if the wording is not clear, if the approval requires a cash payment or signing of a promissory note, or if some of the items listed above are not addressed.

Negotiating A Deficiency Waiver

What happens regarding the deficiency balance is, quite possibly, the most important part of the short sale agreement.

The deficiency balance is the amount you are "short" in your loan repayment after the short sale. For example, if you owe $100,000 to your first lender and $50,000 to your second lender, and the sales proceeds (after commissions and closing costs) only allow you to pay $80,000 to the first lender, and a contribution of $3,500 to the second lender, your deficiency balances would be $20,000 owing to the first, and $46,500 owing to the second.

The aim in any short sale is to negotiate a deficiency waiver. Without a deficiency waiver, it means that you still owe all of that money to your two lenders, even though you do not own the home any more. But if your lenders agree to waive the deficiencies, then they are clearing you of any obligation to ever pay back those loan shortfalls, and you can move forward in your life, free of your old mortgage debt.

It is important that your lender puts the agreement to waive the deficiency balance in writing in your short sale approval letter. Dealing with the deficiency is such an important part of the short sale negotiation process that we are devoting an entire chapter to it: Chapter 14: Deficiency balance, below.

What If The Lender Is Asking For Money On Closing?

A first lender will not normally ask for cash, or signing of a promissory note, in order to agree to the short sale (in non-recourse states, the first lender may not receive that which they would receive by foreclosing, so may not request any cash contribution or promissory note). Junior lenders, also, rarely ask for any funds (cash or promissory note) beyond what the first lender is offering. In particular, if there is clear demonstration of hardship, lenders are unlikely to ask for a cash contribution. Exceptions to this might be:

- if the lenders' review of the last 60 days of bank statements show that the borrower has over $10,000 in savings

- if it is an investment property

- if it is a strategic default.

Usually, the first lender will agree to contribute something towards junior lien-holders in order to close out the loan - usually an amount between $1,000 and about $6,000. Some short sale programs such as HAFA actually provide a fixed amount towards incentives for junior lien-holders. HAFA, for example, provides for a total of up to $8,500 towards junior liens.

Most junior lenders will be satisfied with what the first lender is offering and will grant the approval. Others, particularly credit unions, may be a bit more sticky about their own acceptable minimum proceeds, for example requiring a minimum of 10% or 20% of the balance owing. If the balance owing on a second mortgage is $150,000, the second lender may be holding out for 10% ($15,000), whereas the first lender may not be prepared to give them any more than $6,000. In most cases, the trade-off for meeting that 10% or 20% cash contribution is that the junior lender will then grant a "full settlement," i.e. the borrower is relieved of having to repay the deficiency balance. The junior lender may well settle for less than that (e.g. for the $6,000) but granting only a lien release rather than waiving the deficiency balance.

If the junior lender wants more money than the first lender is offering, this leads to a situation where the second lender requires a cash contribution from the borrower to make up the difference: in the example above, where the first lender is contributing $6,000 that difference would be $9,000. Most financially distressed borrowers do not have that kind of money lying around. (Even cash contributions as small as $500 can be a challenge for a homeowner in financial distress).

Here is another example of where it helps to have professional advice. Depending upon your personal circumstances, it may be better for you to pay the smaller settlement and take your chances as to whether they ever pursue you for the deficiency. But if you expect to be back to work and earning a high wage in a year or two, you might be better off coming up with that extra $9,000 now, rather than take the risk of them pursuing you for that $144,000 deficiency in the future.

Perhaps you can borrow the funds from a friend or relative; perhaps you can put it on your credit card. Perhaps the funds can come from the buyer, to enable the sale to go ahead. For example, if the purchase offer can be restructured so that the offered price is lowered by $9,000, the buyer could agree to bring that $9,000 to closing to cover the excess demand of the junior lien-holder.

If you can somehow come up with the funds, it might just be worth it to meet their demand in order to close the sale. However, having a good financial advisor review your situation is advisable, so you can figure out whether paying that cash contribution makes sense for you both for its short-term and its long-term implications.

If you would like to contribute something to your lender, but simply cannot come up with the cash, then signing a promissory note may be an option.

Should I Sign A Promissory Note?

A promissory note is an unsecured note which is a promise to pay a debt. Unlike your mortgage, where your promise to pay was secured by the home, there is no collateral against an unsecured note.

Lenders who do not waive the deficiency balance may require, as a condition of the short sale, that the borrower sign a promissory note to repay the full balance owing on the loan. In this case, they are not forgiving any of the mortgage debt; they are simply agreeing to release the lien so that the sale of the property may go ahead. Most lenders, though, if they require a promissory note at all, ask for only a portion of the deficiency owing on the loan.

Signing a promissory note can hold many advantages for a borrower who needs the short sale to go ahead. Compared to trying to make a cash payment at a time in your life when you do not have cash, such as the $9,000 in the example above, a promissory note will spread that balance over a long time period such as ten years - often without interest. A $9,000 note, spread over ten years (120 payments) with no interest comes to only $75 per month - a sum that is much more realistic for most people to come up with.

The other advantage of a promissory note is that usually it means that the lender will waive the deficiency, as the new note replaces the old (original) note. In the example above, the balance owing was $150,000. If the first lender contributed $6,000, the deficiency would still be $144,000. If that is not waived, it makes it challenging for a seller to move forward in their life, never knowing whether the debt collectors may one day come knocking at the door. (And the irony is, the more successful the seller is by finding a good job and amassing some savings again, the more likely it is that those debt collectors will come knocking). So paying some small monthly payment on a new promissory note may buy a lot of peace-of-mind, as well as some real financial security moving forward.

A final advantage of the promissory note is that it is an unsecured debt. If things don't work out for the seller, declaring bankruptcy (whether immediately after the short sale, or a few years down the road) is an option. As an unsecured debt, that promissory note will be completely wiped out.

What About Other Lien-Holders?

Other lien-holders are dealt with essentially the same as a second lender. If there are sufficient funds (which usually there are not) they are paid out in the order that the liens are recorded.

If there are not sufficient funds, you must negotiate with all junior lien-holders in order to have them release their lien so the sale can go ahead. Any funds contributed towards junior liens, via HAFA or directly from the first lender's sales proceeds, must be spread out between the juniors. If there are not enough funds to satisfy the juniors' demands, then you may have to make a cash contribution or sign a promissory note to make the deal go ahead.

Negotiating Credit Reporting Language

According to the Federal Trade Commission, negative information, if it is accurate, cannot be removed legally from your credit report. However, it is very important that you review how your short sale has been reported to the credit bureaus, to make sure that reporting is indeed accurate.

If you have become over 120 days delinquent on your mortgage payments, your lender will probably report your account to the credit bureaus as "charged off." This is one of the worst statements that you can receive on a credit report. This means that the lender thinks that it is unlikely that they will ever be able to collect on the debt (and it also gives the lender a tax exemption on the debt) - but it does not mean that you are no longer responsible for repaying the debt.

Once a short sale has been completed, it will normally be reported as "account paid in full with less than full balance" or "legally settled for less than owed." Your approval letter should state in it exactly how you lender is going to report it. It is very important that you check your credit score following a short sale, to make sure that it has been reported correctly.

What If I Don't Like The Deal - Do I Have To Sign?

You absolutely do not have to sign any short sale deal. Make sure that you review all of the details of the short sale approval. By the time you are on the verge of signing off on a short sale, you are probably down to only two options: a short sale, or foreclosure. While for most people a short sale is the best option, for some people foreclosure may still be a better option, for example if your first lender is requiring that you repay a large deficiency balance and simply will not yield.

Make sure that you understand all of the implications of your decision. Pay special attention to the long-term consequences of what you are about to do, in particular:

- how important a good credit rating is to you, for example if you may want to seek financing for a home or other purchase in the future

- what each option means in terms of any deficiency balance(s) you may be responsible for paying

- whether declaring bankruptcy after the short sale, in order to get out of having to repay any deficiencies, might be a wise option for you

- whether you are emotionally prepared to deal with the foreclosure process.

Surround yourself with your professional advisors: your accountant, your attorney, your short sales specialist, and make sure you look at all your options and the consequences of whatever decision you are about to make. If you don't like the deal and what it means to your future, then don't sign it.

Chapter 12

What Is A Deficiency Balance?

The deficiency balance is the difference between what you owe on the loan, and how much you are able to pay back on the loan after selling the home and deducting the closing costs. It is the "short" part of a short sale.

For example, you owe $175,000 on your mortgage, but your home sells for only $150,000. After paying commissions and other closing costs, the sales proceeds to the lender may be only $135,000. This is $40,000 short of what is owed: the deficiency balance (or deficiency) is $40,000.

Possibly the most important part of a short sale agreement, from the seller's perspective, is whether or not they have to repay that deficiency.

How Do I Know Whether I Am Supposed To Repay The Deficiency Balance?

Ideally, your approval letter should spell out whether or not you are responsible for repaying the deficiency. If you have two mortgages, each approval letter should state whether you still owe the deficiency, or whether the lender is waiving you of having to repay the deficiency. Yes, the operative word here is "should." Some lenders are deliberately vague in their wording about the deficiency (or don't mention it altogether). But in some cases, the deficiency is automatically waived.

Some short sales programs do not allow the lender to pursue a deficiency balance. If your short sale is processed through any of the HAFA, FHA, or FHFA short sale programs, your deficiency balance is automatically waived. So sometimes lenders will not state that specifically in the approval letter.

Some states also do not allow lenders to pursue a deficiency balance. Non-recourse states (see Appendix B for a list) do not allow lenders to pursue the deficiency on a first mortgage following foreclosure - so normally, in those states, first lenders will not attempt to pursue the deficiency on a short sale, either. However, the recourse that second lenders (who typically get nothing after a foreclosure) have is to retain their right to pursue the deficiency. Some states also do not allow lenders to pursue a deficiency on a loan that was for purchase money - so it is important that you look up the regulations specific to the state you live in.

If your approval lender does not address the deficiency, you probably have <u>not</u> been waived of having to repay it (unless you short sale was processed through one of the programs mentioned above). If there is no mention of the deficiency, or if the approval letter specifically states that the deficiency has not been waived, you should demand that your lender waive the deficiency and that they reissue the approval letter stating so. Read on to find out how to do that.

Deficiency Language - Sample Wordings

Only a few years ago, the wording in short sale approval letters was all over the place: written in confusing, non-standard language, and often with numerous errors. In the last couple of years, the wording has become much more standardized - at least within any particular lender. Between lenders, though, the wording can be quite different.

Here are some samples of wording from real approval letters.

Deficiency waived:

"Upon receipt of the agreed amount, BAC Home Loans Servicing, LP, and/or its investors will waive the remaining balance due on the above referenced loan and release the borrower from further obligation therein, and waive all rights to pursue further judgment or deficiency. BAC Home Loans Servicing, LP will report the debt as "settled for less than the amount owed" and issue a 1099 for the remaining balance. The seller is encouraged to seek guidance from an independent tax advisor, and/or an attorney, before proceeding with the short sale." (Bank of America)

Accepts sales proceeds "as full and final satisfaction of the first mortgage indebtedness on the above-referenced property." (GMAC)

"As agreed, when we receive the sale proceeds and all required documentation, we will notify the credit bureau to reflect "agreed settlement short of full payment" which would appear on the credit report within 60-90 days from the sale date and within 60-90 days from the date of notification and waive any deficiency rights, if applicable." (Wells Fargo)

"Upon receipt of the required funds, we will release our current lien on the Property and forgive any remaining deficiency balance on the account." (Chase)

"...we agree to issue a Satisfaction of Mortgage." (CMC)

Deficiency not waived:

- "The owner of your mortgage note, the mortgage insurer, if your loan is covered by mortgage insurance, Bank of America, N.A., and their successors and assigns reserve and retain the right to pursue collection of any deficiency following the completion of the short sale, unless otherwise prohibited by law." (Bank of America)

- States that "the lien will be released" but it "reserves the right to collect the remaining balance on your note after application of the net proceeds from the sale." (GMAC)

- Accepts sales proceeds "in order to release Wells Fargo Financial lien on real estate which secures this account. We have agreed to release the lien once the funds are received, but will not consider your account to be paid in full." (Wells Fargo)

Lien release with no mention of deficiency (in other words, it is not explicitly waived):

- Accepts proceeds "in satisfaction of our lien on the property" without mentioning deficiency balance owing (GMAC)

- "Upon receipt of the finds stated above, Wells Fargo Financial agrees to release the lien on this property account number XXXXXXXX." (Wells Fargo)

As you can see, there is no standard deficiency language. So make sure that you read your letter very carefully, and that you understand exactly whether or not you have been waived of having to repay that deficiency.

Beware of confusing language - particularly language which "releases the mortgage" or "discharges the mortgage." This wording is unclear because of the two possible meanings of the word mortgage: mortgage meaning the whole loan (the security interest or lien, plus the deed of trust or promise to pay), or mortgage being just the security interest (the lien only). In contrast, language which "satisfies the mortgage" is usually interpreted as satisfying the whole thing: the lien and the promise to pay the debt associated with it.

If you have any doubts at all about whether your approval actually does waive you of having to repay the deficiency balance, have your attorney review it for you before you agree to the short sale. It is important that you are 100% clear about whether you will still be responsible for any debts following the sale.

What If The Deficiency Is Not Waived?

If the lender has not waived the deficiency, spelled out in clear and unambiguous language, the first thing you should do is contact them and ask them (nicely) to reissue the approval letter with a deficiency waiver. (Remember, if your short sale was processed through

HAFA, FHA or FHFA, or if your mortgage was purchase money in a non-recourse state, the deficiency is automatically waived).

The lender may agree to waive the deficiency only if you agree to either pay a cash contribution upon closing, or sign a promissory note. In that case, you need to look at how much they are wanting you to contribute, and how much the deficiency is, and then evaluate whether or not it is worth it for you to pay. For example, if your deficiency balance is $150,000, and they require you to either pay $5,000 cash or to sign a $10,000 promissory note, it may be worthwhile for you to agree to this because your deficiency is so large: by paying the cash or signing the note, you are permanently getting yourself off the hook. But if the payment they want is high relative to how much the actual deficiency is, it may be worth your while just owing that deficiency, and hoping that they never chase you down for it.

If the lender simply will not waive the deficiency balance, then you must make a decision. Is it still worth it for you to go through with the short sale, when it is possible they will pursue you for the deficiency? For some people, it will still be in their best interests to go through with the sale, and for others it may not be. This again is an example of where it can be really worthwhile for you to be working with a team of professionals who are looking out for your interests and providing you with the best possible advice.

Finally, remember that if the lender does not waive the deficiency, that debt is now an unsecured debt. It is no longer secured against the home. This means that you do have the option of declaring bankruptcy, which will relieve you of the obligation of having to repay any unsecured debts such as deficiency balances. See Chapter 18: Bankruptcy and short sales, below.

Is There A Way To Force The Lender To Waive The Deficiency?

If your lender says that they won't waive the deficiency, you still have some options. In most cases, a lender would rather have a short sale go through than end up owning the property. So you can threaten and let them know that you are not prepared to go through with the short sale if they don't waive the deficiency.

If it is the first lender who won't budge, one option is to let them know you are going to terminate the short sale process and file for bankruptcy. This means that the lender will end up with the property, but nothing else. The other option is to terminate the short sale and just wait for them to foreclose. Again, they will end up with the property (which they probably don't want) and, in non-recourse states, they will not have the right to pursue you for the deficiency.

If it is the second lender who won't waive the deficiency, then you can let them know that you are going to declare bankruptcy after the short sale goes through. The deficiency, as an unsecured debt, will be wiped out by the bankruptcy.

If none of these strategies work, then you will have to make a decision as to whether it is still worth your while to go through with the short sale. People who are forced to go through a short sale do not usually have cash or other assets on hand, and lenders know that. It is quite possible that they will never pursue that deficiency, anyway. You also still have the opportunity to negotiate with your lender after the short sale, to try to settle that deficiency through either a cash payment or a promissory note/payment plan, most likely paying only a small percentage of the total balance owing.

What If The Deficiency Is Waived?

Then give yourself a pat on the back! This is the best outcome - and it is by far the most common outcome for short sale approvals these days.

This means that, once the short sale closes, your mortgage debt is behind you. You don't have to worry about debt collectors pursuing you down the road. You can focus on your future, rather than be haunted by past bad investments.

Chapter 13

Can I Short Sale A Second Or Rental Home?

Can I Short Sale A Second Home?

Yes, you can short sale any property: a second home, a vacation home, a rental home, an investment home. The key to a short sale is simply getting your lender's permission to pay back the mortgage for less than owed before you can go through with the sale.

There are a few things to be aware of, if the property you are selling is not your principal residence. Some short sale programs with incentive payments to the seller may only apply to properties that are the borrower's principal residence. And the taxation rules for forgiven debt may be different if the property is not a principal residence: for more important information on this, see Chapter 17: Tax implications of a short sale, below.

Can I Short Sale A Home That Was Or Is A Rental?

Yes, as mentioned above, you can short sale any property. Some short sale programs, such as FHA, require that the home is owner-occupied, which means that although you can short sale the rental home, you may not be eligible for certain incentives.

The main difference for a rental property is in how any forgiven debt (which is seen by the IRS as income) is reported, since the property was used for generating income. You may be able to offset the forgiven-debt "income" against losses in renting the property. If the property you short sale is a rental, you should definitely work with a tax accounting professional.

What If I Am An "Unintentional Landlord" - When I Bought It, I Planned To Live In It?

For some homeowners, their financial hardship is a result of relocation for work. They could afford their old mortgage payments. But once they were transferred, with property values down and their home underwater, they could not sell the old home - and they needed to pay either rent or mortgage payments on their new home. They had never intended to be landlords, but renting out their old home seemed to be their only option.

Most program guidelines do not look at what your intention with the property was, they just look at when or how long you actually lived in it. The FHA Pre-foreclosure Sale Program does not allow for homes that were purchased as rentals, but does allow for "unintentional" rentals provided that it was not used as a rental for more than 18 months (see below).

The original HAFA program required that the property was owner-occupied at the time of the short sale, or that it had been vacant for no more than 90 days. HAFA guidelines have been revised several times since the program was first introduced. The current guidelines are that a property must not have been vacant for more than 12 months; if it is a rental, the relocation assistance (up to $3,000) payable on closing of the short sale goes to the tenants and not to the borrower/homeowner.

What If I Have Tenants In It?

As long as the rental agreement or lease that you have signed with your tenants does not contain any provision that requires you to give your tenants notice of your intent to sell, you can short sale your rental property without providing notice to the tenants. Exceptions to this would be if your rental agreement states that you must notify the tenants, or if it contains a "subject to tenant's approval" clause such as a "rent-to-own" option.

The new owners of a rental must take the property subject to the existing lease. For some prospective buyers, this could be a reason not to buy - for example if the buyer would like to live in the home shortly after the sale. However, other buyers might find a home that is currently occupied by a renter more attractive, especially those looking to purchase an income-generating investment property.

One wise move for a landlord who is about to list a rental property as a short sale is to renegotiate the lease with the tenant, offering reduced rent in exchange for switching to a month-to-month basis. This can give you the flexibility to negotiate a sale, and also give the tenant sufficient notice so they have time to relocate before the sale closes.

Chapter 14

What Programs And Incentives Are There For Short Sales?

There are numerous short sale programs run both by the government and by the lenders themselves. This section provides a brief overview of the main short sale programs. This information is current as of the time of publication. However, rules and guidelines are frequently revised or amended, so you should check what the most up-to-date rules are for any programs that you think you might qualify for.

FHA Pre-Foreclosure Sale Program

The Federal Housing Administration (FHA) is part of the Department of Housing and Urban Development (HUD). The FHA Pre-foreclosure Sale Program is for homeowners whose mortgages are insured through FHA (typically these are the buyers who were deemed "riskier" buyers, either because of having only a small down payment or a poor credit rating). The rules and guidelines about the FHA Pre-foreclosure Sale Program are outlined in HUD's Mortgagee Letter 2008-43.

The FHA short sale program works by pre-approving a short sale before a buyer is found. The best time to apply to your lender is at the time that your home is listed for sale, if not before. The seller must commit to market the home for four months, and the lender must approve or deny the short sale within five days of receiving a purchase offer.

If the short sale is approved, HUD will pay between $750 and $1,000 to the seller towards relocation costs. HUD will also pay up to $1,500 to help discharge junior liens. The seller can choose to use their relocation incentive towards settling junior liens if necessary, which means that a total of up to $2,500 can be available for settling other liens.

For short sales processed through the FHA program, the first lender is required to waive the deficiency. However, there is no wording in the program guidelines that indicates that junior lenders are required to waive the right to pursue any deficiency.

In order to be eligible for the FHA Pre-foreclosure Sale Program, the property must be an owner-occupied, one-to-four unit single-family dwelling with an FHA-insured mortgage under Title II of the National Housing Act. Investment properties and "walk-away's" are not eligible. Exceptions may be made for rental properties if it is verifiable that the property was not purchased as a rental, that it was not used as a rental for more than 18 months, and that the reason for vacating was related to the cause of default (e.g. job loss or transfer, divorce, death).

Mortgagors must be in default, or soon to be in default, as a result of an adverse and unavoidable situation. Mortgagee Letter 2008-43 notes that "Mortgagees may exercise their discretion to accept applications from mortgagors who are current but facing imminent default." They must be at least 31 days delinquent on their mortgage by the date the short sale closes.

Homeowners must have negative equity in the home. A short sale may be considered if the "as-is" appraised value exceeds the mortgage payoff figure, but gross sales proceeds fall short of the amount required to discharge the mortgage by over $1,000.

You can find and download Mortgagee Letter 2008-43 online.

www.hud.gov/offices/adm/hudclips/letters/mortgagee/files/08-43ml.doc

VA Compromise Sale Program

VA is an abbreviation for the Department of Veterans Affairs. The VA Loan is available to eligible service persons and veterans to help them to negotiate home loans at more favorable terms than most borrowers would have access to. As for FHA, VA does not provide the funds; the mortgage is still issued through a private bank, like any other mortgage. But VA provides a loan guaranty to the lender, promising to pay a specific amount to the lender in case the borrower is unable to continue making payments on their loan.

The VA Compromise Sale Program, often referred to as the VA Short Sales program, is for people who already have a VA loan and who have received a purchase offer that falls short of the amount owing on their loan. VA guarantees a percentage of the loan value, and they will pay the lender the difference between the new purchase price and the amount owing on the VA mortgage, up to the amount that they guaranteed on the original home loan. This makes it much more likely that the lender will approve the short sale.

Completing a short sale through the VA Compromise Sale Program does not necessarily mean that the deficiency balance will be waived.

To qualify for a VA short sale, the seller must demonstrate financial hardship, there must be no other lien on the home (unless the value of that lien is deemed by VA to be "insignificant"), and the cost of the short sale must be less to VA than what the cost of foreclosure would be.

Details of the program can be found in the brochure called "Department of Veterans Affairs Compromise Sale Program" which you can download online http://www.benefits.va.gov/roanoke/RLC/forms/COMP-SALEProgramTrainingVaBeach.pdf

1-800-603-3525

HAFA

The Home Affordable Foreclosure Alternative program (HAFA) was introduced by the federal government in April 2010, in an attempt to slow the growing wave of foreclosures by making the short sale process more streamlined and standardized. It was also made attractive to both homeowners and lenders by offering cash incentives to both.

The HAFA program has been amended several times. At the time of writing, the HAFA program is scheduled to run through 2014. The HAFA short sale must be initiated by December 31, 2013, and the transaction must close before September 30, 2014. Check with your short sales specialist, or with the government Making Home Affordable website, for the most current guidelines and deadlines. http://www.makinghomeaffordable.gov/programs/exit-gracefully/pages/hafa.aspx

As of the June 1, 2012 amendments, HAFA pays a cash incentive of $3,000 to the homeowner (or to the occupant, if not owner-occupied) upon closing of a short sale. The relocation incentive will not be paid if the property is unoccupied. HAFA also offers the primary loan servicer $1,500 for closing the short sale, and up to $8,500 to settle any junior liens.

The most important part of the HAFA program - even more significant than the cash incentives offered - is that none of the lenders may pursue the borrower for the deficiency balance after closing of a HAFA short sale. The HAFA program also provides specific deadlines by which the lender must respond to the borrower's short sale application.

The original version of HAFA required that the homeowner was the occupant of the property, and that the homeowner's monthly mortgage payment exceeds 31% of the borrower's gross income; both of these eligibility requirements have been discontinued.

HAFA eligibility requirements that are still in place are:

- the mortgage lien must be a first lien mortgage originated on or before January 1, 2009.

- the mortgage must be delinquent, or default is reasonably foreseeable.

- the current unpaid principal balance must be equal to or less than $729,750.

If the borrower's loan is backed by VA or FHA, they must apply through one of those short sales programs rather than through HAFA.

You can find out more information about HAFA, including any recent changes to eligibility requirements, by visiting http://www.makinghomeaffordable.gov/programs/exit-gracefully/Pages/hafa.aspx.

FHFA "Standard Short Sale" Program

The Federal Housing and Finance Agency (FHFA) announced new guidelines that apply to mortgage loans where the investors are the GSE's FHLMC (Freddie Mac) and FNMA (Fannie Mae) and which took effect on November 1, 2012. Their new "standard short sale" program is similar to HAFA, and replaced their involvement in HAFA.

Freddie and Fannie will offer up to $3,000 in relocation costs and up to $8,500 to settle with junior lien-holders. It is important to note that, in this program, the relocation incentive is total: if, for example, a homeowner receives $2,000 towards relocation from another source, such as their employer, Freddie or Fannie will only offer the $1,000 difference to make up the $3,000.

As long as the borrower has negotiated in good faith with their lender, Freddie or Fannie will waive them of having to repay the deficiency balance.

The FHFA program, like HAFA, is aimed at streamlining the short sale process by requiring lenders to meet specific deadlines in responding to a short sale request. An important and new aspect of the FHFA program is that it gives lenders more authority to approve short sales, without taking the case to the investor and to the mortgage insurer, provided that basic eligibility requirements are met.

In order to be eligible for the FHFA "standard short sale" program, a borrower must either be 31 or more days delinquent on their mortgage payments, or they must have undergone one of four eligible hardships. The eligible hardships are:

- divorce or separation

- death of the borrower or the primary wage earner

- long-term permanent disability of the borrower or dependent family member

- distant employment transfer or relocation (including PCS for service members).

For borrowers who are 31 or more days delinquent, all property types are eligible for the servicer-approved "standard short sale" - including primary residences, investment properties, and second homes. However, for borrowers who are current or less than 31 days delinquent, the home must be their primary residence, and their monthly debt-to-income ratio must be greater than 55% (service member with PSC orders are exempt from this last requirement).

If a borrower does not meet the criteria above, they are not eligible for the "standard short sale," but their lender may still forward their file to Freddie or Fannie to consider approval under the "traditional short sale" program.

For more information on the FHFA Standard Short Sale, refer to: http://www.fhfa.gov/webfiles/24211/Shortsales82112Final.pdf

Lender Short Sale Programs And Incentives

Some of the lenders themselves have their own short sale programs. Information on these in-house programs is sometimes difficult to come by, as lenders treat them as "invitation-only" programs to borrowers who they see as at-risk.

Some of the lenders' in-house programs may pay cash incentives that are substantially higher than the $3,000 on offer by HAFA or FHFA. The incentives are this high - sometimes as much as $20,000 to $35,000 - because it is cheaper for lenders to pay this kind of incentive than it is for them to go through with a foreclosure. These high incentives are more likely to be offered in states where foreclosures take a longer time.

Although these are not generally programs you can apply to, it is worth trying your luck by asking your lender if there are any in-house short sale programs that they don't advertise that they may consider you for. Here is an overview of some of the lenders' programs.

Bank of America Cooperative Sale Program. This program began as a test program in Florida in early 2012, and it is now available to select borrowers in other states as well. Incentives to homeowners reportedly range from $2,500 to $30,000. It is only available to homeowners who apply before submitting a purchase offer through Bank of America's short sale processing Equator system. If you want to try to qualify for this program, you should start working with a short sale specialist at the time of listing your home, or even before.

Wells Fargo. Wells Fargo reportedly offers cash incentives ranging from less than $3,000 to $20,000 to homeowners for closing a short sale.

Chase. Chase offers cash incentives of up to $35,000 to homeowners for completing a short sale. You cannot apply for the Chase incentive; they may send letters out to distressed homeowners offering them an incentive of a specified amount for completing a short sale.

The cash incentive may be listed in the short sale approval. However, in some cases it is not mentioned in the approval letter, and listed only in the lender's financial worksheet.

Double-Dipping On Cash Incentives

In many cases you may "double-dip" on cash incentives - for example, if a short sale incentive is offered by your lender, and you also process the short sale through HAFA. But make sure that you read the approval letter and the HUD sheet carefully so you understand exactly what your lender is offering: some lenders will allow you to "stack" the incentives, while others may indicate that the $3,000 HAFA incentive is included within their offered incentive.

Some lenders may even offer you a cash incentive for closing the deal, in addition to some cash towards relocation expenses.

Also keep in mind that the FHFA incentive of $3,000 towards relocation expenses is a total amount. If anyone else, such as an employer, is offering funds towards relocation expenses, this does not "stack." FHFA will allow only up to a total of $3,000 for relocation, so they will not pay you that full amount if you are already receiving relocation funds from another party.

Chapter 15

What Are The Tax Implications Of Doing A Short Sale?

There are tax implications for borrowers following the short sale of their home. IRS Publication 4681 provides detailed information on how you can be exempted from having to pay income tax on forgiven debt. It is advisable to work with a good tax accountant, to minimize your tax obligations.

Do I Have To Pay Tax On Forgiven Mortgage Debt?

The IRS normally considers any forgiven debt as taxable income. For example, if you owe $250,000 on your mortgage, and you negotiate a short sale where you pay your lender $200,000, if your lender waives you of having to repay that $50,000 deficiency balance, the IRS normally considers that $50,000 to be "income" and taxable.

For a person who has just completed a short sale and no longer owns the home, paying income tax on monies that they never actually received is probably impossible. Fortunately, the federal government has realized that, and has come up with some exemptions for homeowners who have had mortgage debt forgiven, described below.

Mortgage Forgiveness Debt Relief Act Of 2007

The Mortgage Forgiveness Debt Relief Act of 2007 became law in December 2007. It has so far been extended twice, and is currently in effect until December 31, 2013. The Act was passed in recognition of the special economic circumstances of the global financial crisis, as a special provision to relieve struggling homeowners of having to pay income tax on any forgiven mortgage debt (including debt forgiven through short sales, foreclosure, or loan modifications).

To qualify, the debt must have been forgiven by the current expiration date of December 31, 2013. Other eligibility requirements are:

- The maximum amount you can treat as qualified principal residence indebtedness is $2 million, or $1 million if married and filing separately.

- The forgiven debt must have been used to buy, build, or substantially improve the residence. In other words, forgiven debt on both first and second mortgages can be included under the Act provided that the debt was used for one of those purposes - but not if it was used for other purposes, e.g. to pay off credit cards or to buy a new car.

- The forgiven debt must be secured by that same residence.

Refinanced debt proceeds may also qualify for exclusion under the Act, provided that they were used to "substantially improve" the residence and not for other purposes.

If your lender forgives more than $600 of debt, they are required by law to issue you with a 1099-C Cancellation of Debt form. It is important that you check the form for accuracy as soon as you receive it. If you qualify for tax relief from the Mortgage Forgiveness Debt Relief Act, fill out IRS Form 982, and attach it to your income tax return.

Insolvency

Unlike the Mortgage Forgiveness Debt Relief Act of 2007, there is no expiration date to apply for tax relief through the insolvency clause: this is a permanent exemption, regardless of when your short sale took place or when your lender forgave your mortgage debt.

Insolvency means that the total value of all of your liabilities is greater than the total value of all of your assets. Your assets are everything you <u>own</u>: the value of your real estate properties, your bank account balances, your investments and retirement savings, and the fair market value of anything else you own such as cars, tools, jewelry, books, etc. (Fair market value means the price you could sell them for today, not what you paid for them). Your liabilities mean all of your <u>debts</u>: your mortgages, your car loans, your credit card debts, any student loans or medical bills owed, etc. The IRS has an insolvency worksheet that you can use to calculate all of this.

If the value of all your debts (everything you owe) is greater than the value of all your assets (everything you own), then you are insolvent. If you were insolvent on the date that your debt was forgiven, you will not have to pay income tax on some or all of that forgiven debt.

Whether you have to pay any income tax at all depends upon the "extent of your insolvency" relative to the amount of debt that was forgiven. For example, if you use the insolvency worksheet, and calculate that (on the date your debt was forgiven) you owed $80,000 more than what all your assets were worth, this means that you were insolvent by $80,000. This is the extent of your insolvency.

If the amount of debt that your lender forgave is less than the extent of your insolvency, then it does not bring you up to solvency and that forgiven debt it not taxable at all. So, if your lender forgave $60,000 of debt, you are still insolvent by $20,000. The forgiven debt does not bring you up to solvency, so none of that forgiven debt is taxable.

However, if the lender forgave $90,000 of debt, then this brings you up to solvency. Only the $10,000 that is beyond bringing you to solvency will be taxable. That $10,000 will be added to your earned income for that year, and taxed at the appropriate rate.

The insolvency clause applies to any forgiven debt, not just mortgage debt. If your debt has been cancelled through insolvency, attach Form 982 to your income tax return.

Other Exemptions

There are other exemptions that homeowners who have had mortgage debt forgiven might be able to use to avoid paying income tax on the forgiven debt. The most common one is bankruptcy: any debt forgiven through Title 11 bankruptcy is not taxable. Title 11 bankruptcy includes Chapters 7, 11 and 13 bankruptcy, provided that the debtor is under the jurisdiction of the court and the cancellation of the debt is granted by the court, or occurs as a result of a plan approved by the court. If your debt has been cancelled through bankruptcy, attach Form 982 to your income tax return.

Other exemptions that exempt you from paying income tax on forgiven debt, but that are unlikely to apply to a short sale situation, include qualified farm indebtedness and qualified real property business indebtedness. If you believe that your debt qualifies for exclusion from paying income tax through either of these clauses, you should read IRS Publication 4681 as well as speak to a qualified tax accountant.

Are Incentive Payments Taxable?

Incentive payments, whether through a government short sale program or through a lender's in-house program, will normally be taxable as income. They may not be exempted through the Mortgage Forgiveness Debt Relief Act of 2007, but they may qualify for exclusion through the insolvency exemption. Check with your tax account.

Chapter 16

How Are Bankruptcy And Short Sales Related?

Bankruptcy and short sales can work hand in hand. Bankruptcy is a strategic move that can be undertaken before, during, or after a short sale. While bankruptcy is not for everyone, for some people it is the fastest and most secure route for shedding debts and getting a clean new start on life. The evaluation processes for a short sale and for bankruptcy are very similar, so it is wise to consider both options before coming up with a final plan. Advice from experienced professionals in coming up with an appropriate plan may save you thousands of dollars or more.

A Brief Explanation Of Bankruptcy

Many people are afraid of the idea of declaring bankruptcy, but this is often because they don't understand what declaring bankruptcy actually means. They fear bankruptcy because they believe it means losing everything they own. In reality, though, most people who declare bankruptcy don't lose anything at all.

Declaring bankruptcy means assessing a current financial situation, and taking charge of it. Most people end up being able to exempt their assets and keeping everything they own. In Chapter 7 bankruptcy, assets such as jewelry, tools of the trade, their car, and even their house may be exempted. Chapter 13 bankruptcy usually involves coming up with modified payment plans for assets such as home or car, rather than liquidating (selling) assets; however, both can be used to obtain more time in order to complete loan modifications or sales of these assets.

Declaring bankruptcy stops a foreclosure proceeding immediately. As part of the Bankruptcy Code, the moment a petition for bankruptcy is filed, the court imposes an "automatic stay" which stops the commencement, enforcement or appeal of most actions or judgments against the debtor. It also prohibits any collection actions, such as a foreclosure, against the estate. Filing for bankruptcy will allow you to keep your home - at least for the period that the stay is in place, and possibly permanently. This extra time may be just what you need in order to negotiate a short sale.

How long the foreclosure process is stopped for depends upon which type of bankruptcy you have filed for. Generally, Chapter 7 only provides a temporary stop to the foreclosure process. Even if the lender does not file the request for relief, usually the case and the stay will end approximately 120 days from the date of filing. Depending upon how much equity you have in your home, you may be able to keep your home by reaffirming your mortgage (which stops the foreclosure), so your home remains outside of the bankruptcy proceeding.

Chapter 13 bankruptcy can stop the foreclosure for a longer period of time. You must then either come up with a payment plan, get a modification done, or short sell the home. Filing for Chapter 13 bankruptcy only protects you from foreclosure as long as you are adhering to the terms of the new plan. For secured debts, such as your mortgage, you must immediately begin making your monthly payments, and the amount of mortgage payments you are late on will be considered "priority unsecured debt" which will have to be paid in full as part of your payment plan. If you miss your payments, your lender may ask for relief from the automatic stay and resume foreclosure proceedings.

Bankruptcy will affect your credit score, but it may not hit as hard as you think. In fact, declaring bankruptcy can actually raise your credit score! This can happen in two ways. Most people who are considering bankruptcy have very high debt loads, and those late payments and unpaid balances drag their credit score down. But once they declare bankruptcy, this information is removed and marked "Included in Chapter 7 Bankruptcy" or "Included in Chapter 13 Wage Earner Plan." Also, credit score is calculated partly by comparing with other people in similar situations. When your score is calculated in comparison with other people who have declared bankruptcy, it can actually make your finances appear better.

It is also easier to rebuild credit score after declaring bankruptcy than if you did not. This is because, after bankruptcy, your outstanding debts are no longer considered delinquent.

For most distressed homeowners, choosing a short sale and/or declaring bankruptcy are preferable options to foreclosure. Bankruptcy creates a plan for dealing with all debts, not just mortgage debt. Chapter 7 bankruptcy allows unsecured debts, such as credit cards, to be completely wiped. In some cases, Chapter 13 bankruptcy may allow for "lien stripping": having undersecured junior liens (e.g. in underwater homes) become considered as unsecured debts, so that only a portion of them must be repaid. Once other debts are either removed or diminished, paying a first mortgage and keeping a home may suddenly become more manageable. Alternatively, for others, combining a short sale with bankruptcy may be the best option for clearing all debts and moving directly on to a new financial start.

Keeping Your Home Through Bankruptcy

Since the evaluation processes for a short sale and for bankruptcy are nearly the same, it is worth investigating the possibility of not doing a short sale at all. Some people will find that they can declare bankruptcy and keep their home!

If you have less than a certain amount of equity in your home (that number will vary state by state), one option you have is to declare Chapter 7 bankruptcy, but reaffirm your mortgage(s). This means that you declare bankruptcy to shed your other debts, but you affirm your commitment to continue to pay your mortgage(s). Your home and mortgage will be unaffected by the proceeding. The mortgage debt survives the bankruptcy (in other words you must continue to pay it) and you keep the home.

This can be a good move for someone who is overwhelmed with other unsecured debts, such as credit card debt or medical bills, but who is earning enough income that they would be able to afford their mortgage payments if only those other debts could be made to disappear. However, if you own more than the amount of equity set by your state in your home, this may not be an option for you. Then you may be forced to include the home in the bankruptcy, and surrender the home to the trustee. Alternatively, you may pay cash to the bankruptcy estate to cover this difference. If you do surrender your home, you will receive that state-set amount of equity back from the sales proceeds following the sale.

You can also declare Chapter 13 bankruptcy and keep your home. Chapter 13 bankruptcy is debt restructuring, so you would have to be prepared to make your normal mortgage payments, as well as come up with a plan with your lender whereby you make up your missed payments over a period of three or five years.

"Riding Through" A Bankruptcy

One option that may be available in some states is to "ride through" the bankruptcy. The borrower notes their intention to have the debt discharged through bankruptcy while continuing to occupy the home. It is a strange kind of middle-ground, where they are no longer technically responsible for the mortgage debt, but they must continue to make mortgage payments to their lender in order to assert their right to occupy the property.

Most states have disallowed the option of borrowers "riding through" without reaffirming their debt. Check with a bankruptcy lawyer to find out if this is an option in your state.

Declaring Bankruptcy Before Initiating The Short Sale Process

If you have chosen to ride through a bankruptcy, you can stay in the home as long as you continue to make your mortgage payments. You still have title to the home - but, if you decide that you want to move, you are stuck. You can't sell the home. But as soon as you stop making the mortgage payments, your lender will foreclose on you.

One option, to avoid the black mark of a foreclosure on your credit report, is to work with your lender to negotiate a short sale. This way you and your lender can mutually agree to terminate the mortgage, and you can exit with little additional damage to your credit score.

Declaring Bankruptcy And Doing A Short Sale Together

Chapter 13 bankruptcy is considered to be debt restructuring. Aside from trying to work a loan modification or repayment plan with your lender, you also have the option of trying to negotiate a short sale. Your lender will usually give you six or so months to negotiate the short sale while in Chapter 13 bankruptcy.

Title to the property remains in the borrower's name until the short sale is closed. The lender(s) must then waive the deficiency balance and, since that debt was discharged through bankruptcy, the borrower is exempt from having to pay any income tax on the forgiven debt.

Declaring Bankruptcy After A Short Sale

Declaring Chapter 7 bankruptcy immediately following a short sale makes sense if your lender has refused to waive a large deficiency balance. Before the short sale, the mortgage was secured by the home, but after the short sale, with no home as collateral, the deficiency is now an unsecured debt. Unsecured debts can be completely shed through Chapter 7 bankruptcy.

Theoretically, you could wait a number of years to declare Chapter 7 bankruptcy in order to have the deficiency judgment shed. However, there are income limits for being able to declare Chapter 7. If you think your income may be higher in the future than it is now (e.g., if your financial distress was caused by unemployment or under-employment, but you think you might be back to regular work in a few years) you would be better off to declare Chapter 7 bankruptcy right away after the short sale, while you are still eligible for it.

Bankruptcy Strategies

There are numerous ways that you can use the various types of bankruptcy in combination, or bankruptcy and a short sale, to your best financial advantage. Everyone's circumstances are different, so it is important that you get good advice from accountants and a good bankruptcy attorney.

For example, as mentioned above, you can do a short sale, and then declare Chapter 7 bankruptcy immediately after in order to shed yourself of any obligation to repay the deficiency balance.

You can also use Chapter 7 or Chapter 13 bankruptcy to temporarily stop the foreclosure process, which might just give you enough time to negotiate a short sale. In Chapter 7 that stop may be fairly short, but in Chapter 13 bankruptcy your lender will usually allow you around 6 months to find a buyer and negotiate a short sale.

The advice of a knowledgeable and experienced professional can be invaluable in coming up with a strategic plan. For example, for some people, short-selling a home followed by Chapter 7 bankruptcy can result in shedding of any deficiency balances owing along with all other unsecured debts, such as credit cards. For others, it would be more advantageous to first enter Chapter 13 and then short-sale the home. Bankruptcy lawyers and other professionals can provide advice specific to each individual financial situation and to the homeowner's specific goals.

Chapter 17

Who Are The People Buying Short Sales?

Who Are The People Buying Short Sales?

Short sales, as "distressed property sales," generally come on the market for a slightly lower asking price than comparable properties being sold as traditional real estate sales. This is because short sales are on a tight timeline: if they do not secure a buyer and finalize the sale within a fixed time period, the lender will move forward with foreclosure. The asking price needs to be low enough to generate an offer quickly.

This means that the people buying short sales are usually people looking for real estate deals. Many short sale buyers are experienced real estate investors, who understand the short sale process and the delays and uncertainties that go with it. But some are first-time buyers who are looking for a starter home, and who are hoping to get a good deal but who do not understand the complexities of a short sale, or that there is the possibility of delays or of the deal not closing.

How Can I Work With Them?

In most cases, the seller has no direct contact with the buyers. Communications between buyer and seller are done through the real estate agents, and possibly also through a specialist short sale negotiator.

There are a few things you can do, though, to make your home attractive to buyers and to facilitate a sale:

- Keep the utilities connected. It is hard for a prospective buyer to view a place, not to mention to have appraisals and inspections done, if the power and the water are off.

- Disclose all defects up front to your buyer (through your real estate agent and your short sale negotiator) so they can put together an offer that reflects the true value of the home. Finding out that something is wrong only after an offer has been approved may cause the whole deal to fall through.

The more your home looks like a warm and welcoming and cared-for home, the more likely you are to attract a serious buyer who will pay a fair price for it (see Section 12.9: Preparing your home to show, above). A cluttered or uncared-for home, in contrast, may attract more difficult buyers, who are really just pushing for a rock-bottom deal.

Chapter 18

Scams To Watch Out For

There are more than a few scams out there, regarding so-called "credit repair" and loan modifications, and also specifically oriented towards short sales. It definitely pays to do your homework and find out for yourself what is and isn't allowed. In general, be suspicious of anyone who approaches you with a deal of how to save your home.

Specialist short sales negotiators can protect you from scams, but be sure to research any company that you are considering working with. Make sure that they are legitimate, and that they have a proven track record of short sales that they have closed that you can verify.

Here are some of the common short sales scams to be wary of:

Simultaneous buyers. This is a scam that some unscrupulous real estate agents have undertaken, usually without the knowledge of the seller. And it is fraud. In this scam, the agent presents you with a purchase offer - but, unknown to you, he has another buyer who has offered a higher purchase price. You sign the deal with the agent's "straw buyer," and he closes both deals the same day, pocketing the difference in purchase price. Many lenders now have provisions in their short sale approvals that do not allow simultaneous buyers, in order to prevent this type of fraud. For example, FHFA guidelines do not allow a home that has been sold through a short sale to be resold for 30 days, or to be resold for more than 120% of the short sale purchase price for 90 days.

Seller's straw buyer. This is an idea that many people who are underwater with their mortgages and faced with the prospect of foreclosure come up with - but beware, it is fraud. This is where the seller has their own "straw buyer," usually a friend or a relative. The idea is that they get their lender's approval for a short sale to the straw buyer, with a sales price that is less than the amount owing on their mortgage, then at some point they purchase the home back from the straw buyer at that reduced price.

For example, if a seller owes $300,000 on their mortgage, but their home is now only valued at $200,000, they may want to short sale their home to a relative for $200,000. Through the short sale, they shed that $300,000 mortgage debt. Then, in the future, they get financing to re-purchase the home back from their relative for $200,000. While this may appear to be a good way to keep your home while knocking $100,000 off your mortgage balance, it is fraud. A lender approves a short sale on the condition that the seller is not to benefit from that sale.

This is why lenders normally have an "arm's length transaction" requirement on short sales. They may also require you to sign an "occupancy agreement," stating that you or any close family member may not live in the home after the sale.

Leaseback scams. Some scammers will contact you, promising that if you sign your house over to them, they will rent the house back to you while they negotiate the short sale. They then collect that rent money for you, while they delay on getting that short sale negotiated, until finally the house is foreclosed upon and you are booted out - while the scammer collected all that rent money from you. Alternatively, they do succeed at negotiating the short sale, after collecting all that rent money from you - and you are still booted out. Do not sign your house over to anyone: there are legitimate short sale negotiators out there, but they will never ask you to sign your home over.

Chapter 19

The Short Sale As A Move To Freedom

Short sales are not the only way to avoid foreclosure, and they may not be the best move for everyone. But an increasing number of Americans are finding that a short sale is their surest and fastest route to financial freedom. The fiascos with the whole loan modification process have resulted in the number of completed loan modifications dropping by over one half between 2009 and 2012. Meanwhile, over that same period, the number of short sales has steadily grown.

There is good reason that short sales continue to become increasingly popular with both borrowers and lenders. For borrowers, a short sale represents a final and permanent end to their mortgage struggles. In the majority of short sales, deficiencies on mortgage balances are waived, which means the borrower sheds all of their mortgage debt, forever - while avoiding the stress and stigma (not to mention the hard hit to the credit score) that foreclosure brings. And for lenders, a short sale usually represents their best loss mitigation tactic: an effective way to minimize their losses on a non-performing loan. A short sale is a win for both sides.

If you are concerned about your ability to continue making your mortgage payments, or if you are already delinquent on your mortgage, it is important that you start working on a solution right away. Surround yourself with competent advisors, including lawyers, accountants, real estate agents, and short sale specialists. Do your research. Get informed about all of your options, and whether there are any state-specific regulations that apply to you, so you can work out which strategy suits your unique situation best.

Then, take action. You may find, like thousands of other Americans have, that a short sale is your surest and fastest route to financial freedom.

Appendix A:

Glossary Of Terms

Adjustable rate mortgage: Also called a "balloon mortgage." A mortgage with a lower "teaser" interest rate for the first two years. The interest rate typically resets to a higher rate after two or three years. See also "Option ARM."

Agency: The relationship, as outlined in a written contract, between the sellers or buyers of a property and their realtor. It outlines the realtor's obligations and duties to the client.

Agent: In the context of real estate, a person who acts as an intermediary between the buyer and the sellers when negotiating a real estate transaction. Usually one agent works on behalf of the buyer, and another on behalf of the seller. Agents are usually paid a commission which is a percentage of the property sales price. A real estate agent may not work independently; they must work through a broker. See also broker.

A-loan: A mortgage loan to a highly qualified, low-risk borrower. Typically, this requires a credit score of 700 or higher. Also called a prime mortgage.

Alt-A loan: A mortgage loan to a borrower who does not quite meet the A-loan standard.

ARM: See "adjustable rate mortgage."

Arm's-length transaction: A requirement, usually by the lender, that the buyer and seller are unrelated and unaffiliated by family, marriage, or commercial enterprise. This requirement is sometimes extended to other parties to the transaction: buyer's agent, seller's agent, third-party negotiators.

Authorization letter: A letter from the homeowner to their foreclosing lender authorizing it to talk to third parties about the seller's short sale file.

Borrower: An entity that borrows money.

BPO: See "broker's price opinion."

Broker: A higher level of real estate agent, usually because they have a higher level of education and have passed a broker's real estate exam. See also agent.

Broker's Price Opinion: A statement of opinion undertaken by a broker as to the fair market value of a property.

Capital: See "down payment".

Closing costs: Fees paid in a real estate transaction, e.g. realtor's commissions, etc. In a traditional sale, these are normally paid by the buyer or seller. In a short sale, these are normally paid by the lender out of the sales proceeds.

CMA: See "Comparative Market Analysis"

Collateral: The property that secures the loan. In a home mortgage, the collateral is the home.

Commission: In the context of real estate, the fee that real estate agents earn upon the closing of a property sale. This is normally calculated as between 5 and 6% of the sales price, and it is normally split between the buyer's agent and the seller's agent. In some sales the commission may be negotiable.

Comparative Market Analysis: An analysis by a listing agent ,which shows what homes similar to the property being listed have sold for in that same neighborhood, as well as what other comparable homes are currently priced at. It is used to provide guidance in the listing price of the home.

Credit score: A number that reflects a borrower's track record in meeting repayment obligations on previous loans or debts. Credit scores range from 300 to 900, with the majority of people in the 600 to 800 range. Most lenders consider a credit score above around 700 to be good, and a score under about 620 to reflect a risky borrower.

Credit history: A record of your history of borrowing and repaying debts.

Credit report: A complete and confidential summary of your credit history including your existing debts and how well you've repaid past debts. A credit report will also usually contain confidential information about you, such as your social security number and your current and previous address, as well as a list of companies that have inquired about your credit history.

Debt forgiveness: See "forgiven debt."

Deed in lieu of foreclosure: The borrower choosing to deed their property back to the lender. Also known as "voluntary foreclosure."

Deed of trust: A type of promissory note, where a third party (the Trustee) holds title to the lien for the benefit of the lender. Also called a trust deed.

Default: In mortgages, when a borrower fails to make their mortgage payment.

Deficiency: (Also known as "deficiency balance.") The amount of the shortfall, when paying off a mortgage for less than the amount owing, after a short sale or foreclosure.

Deficiency judgment: A court order permitting the lender to collect the deficiency from the borrower.

Deficiency waiver: A written statement from the lender indicating that they will not attempt to collect the deficiency. In a short sale, the deficiency waiver is normally written into the short sale approval letter.

Delinquent: When an account is past due (i.e. one or payments have been missed).

DIL: See "Deed in lieu of foreclosure."

Equity: The proportion of the property that the homeowner actually owns (i.e. the probable selling price of the property minus the amount owing on the property mortgage). See also "Negative equity."

Fair market value: The price that a seller could reasonably be expected to sell at, and that a buyer could fairly be expected to pay, on the current open market.

Fannie Mae: The Federal National Mortgage Association, or FNMA, which is a government-sponsored enterprise that purchases mortgages from lenders in order to increase the amount of mortgage funds available to borrowers.

FHA: The Federal Housing Administration, a part of HUD which helps provide mortgage insurance on loans made by FHA-approved lenders.

Financial statement: A document which shows a person's total assets and total liabilities, as well as their net worth.

FMV: See "fair market value."

Forbearance: One type of loan modification: where a lender temporarily suspends payments. Usually, the borrower must make up those missed payments later.

Foreclosure: A legal process by which the lender or creditor seizes property that was used as collateral for a mortgage or debt, usually due to the homeowner not making timely payments on the mortgage or debt.

Forgiven debt: Any amount owing on a loan that the lender has waived the borrower of having to repay. Usually this is the deficiency following a foreclosure or a short sale; it may also include other amounts that are forgiven, such as through principal reduction in a loan modification.

Freddie Mac: A short form for the Federal Home Loan Mortgage Corporation (FHMLC), a government-sponsored enterprise that buys mortgages on the secondary market, pools them, and sells them as mortgage-backed securities to investors on the open market.

Government-sponsored enterprise: A financial services corporation created by the federal government, with the intended functions of enhancing the flow of credit to targeted sectors of the economy.

GSE: See "Government sponsored enterprise."

HAMP: The Home Affordable Modification Program, a program set up by the federal government to assist distressed homeowners in negotiating loan modifications with their lenders.

HAFA: The Home Affordable Foreclosure Alternatives Program, a program set up by the federal government with similar eligibility criteria to HAMP, to assist homeowners and lenders in processing short sales.

HOA: See "Homeowners Association."

Homeowners Association: A legal entity created to maintain common areas, frequently used to manage communal living developments such as townhouses and condominiums.

HUD: The Department of Housing and Urban Development, a federal agency responsible for encouraging housing development.

HUD-1: A document that accounts for closing costs and all payoffs of liens upon settlement of a real estate transaction. Also known as a settlement statement or closing statement.

Hardship letter: Part of the short sale package, a letter the borrower writes to the lender explaining the circumstances (usually decreased income or increased expenses) that have led to them being unable to repay their mortgage.

Investor: The owner of the loan. Most mortgage loans are sold by the originator of the loan (usually a bank) to an investor such as Freddie Mac or Fannie Mae. See also servicer.

Judicial (sale, foreclosure): A foreclosure or trustee sale that is processed through the court system. See also "non-judicial." A list of judicial states is included as Appendix C.

Lender: An entity that loans money. This is a vague term, since usually the loan is sold by the originator or servicer of the loan to an investor.

Lien: When a lien is placed on a consumer's property, it means the property is being used as collateral during the repayment of owed money. A consumer cannot sell a property with a lien on it until they have paid off the creditor with whom they have the lien.

Loan-mod: See "loan modification."

Loan modification: A permanent adjustment made to one or more of the terms of a borrower's existing loan, negotiated between the borrower and the lender. (Also called "mortgage modification.")

Loan servicer: See "servicer."

Loan-to-value ratio: The ratio of how much a purchaser wants to borrow relative to the purchase price of a home. For example, if the purchase price of a home is $200,000 and the borrower needs to borrow $150,000, the loan-to-value ratio is 75%.

Loss mitigation committee: A lender's department that tries to reduce the lender's losses from bad mortgages. Usually the loss mitigation committee has the authority to approve short sales.

LTV: See "loan-to-value ratio."

MI: See "mortgage insurance."

Mortgage: A loan taken to purchase "real property," where that property is pledged as collateral for the loan.

Mortgage insurance: An insurance policy that compensates lenders or investors for losses if the borrower defaults on their loan.

Mortgage modification: See "loan modification."

Mortgagee: The lender in a mortgage.

Mortgagor: The borrower in a mortgage.

Negative equity: When a borrower owes more on their mortgage(s) than the property is worth. See also "equity."

Negotiator: May refer to the negotiator working on behalf of the lender, who communicates the decision as to whether the short sale is approved or not, or to a negotiator working on behalf of the borrower. See also "Short sale negotiator."

NOD: See "Notice of Default."

Non-judicial (sale, foreclosure): Foreclosure without going through the courts, only permitted in some states. Refer to Appendix C for a list of non-judicial states. See also "judicial."

Non-performing mortgage: A mortgage in which the borrower is behind on payments.

Notice of Default: A letter from the lender officially letting a homeowner know that they are behind in their mortgage payments, and that the lender is beginning the foreclosure process.

Option ARM: An adjustable rate mortgage where the borrower has the option of paying a lower, interest-only, monthly mortgage payment, or of paying even less than the monthly interest. These mortgages typically reset after two or three years: the borrower will then no longer have the option of making the lower monthly payment (and their interest rate may also have reset to a higher rate as well). Option ARMs contributed to the wave of foreclosures in 2008, as mortgages issued in 2005 and 2006 reset to higher monthly payments that homeowners could not afford.

Owner's Right of Redemption: Only permitted in some states, a statute that allows homeowners who have been foreclosed upon to purchase their property back. Normally only an option for six to twelve months after a foreclosure, and not available after a short sale. Also known as "equity of redemption."

Performing mortgage: A mortgage in which the borrower is keeping current on payments.

PMI: Private mortgage insurance. See "mortgage insurance."

Prime mortgage: A mortgage loan to a highly qualified, low-risk borrower. Typically, this requires a credit score of 700 or higher. Also called an A-loan.

Processor: A person working for the lender who processes the documentation and makes sure nothing is missing, before passing the file on to the negotiator.

PSA: See "Purchase and Sale Agreement."

Purchase and Sale Agreement: A legal contract by which a buyer makes a purchase offer on a property, and by which the buyer and seller may counter and negotiate terms. The agreement only becomes binding when both buyer and seller have signed an identical copy of it.

Real-estate owned: Refers to properties that banks and mortgage companies have foreclosed on and subsequently purchased through the foreclosure auction

Reinstatement of mortgage: The borrower's right, when delinquent on mortgage payments and facing foreclosure, to pay all overdue payments, plus any penalties or late fees, in order to stop the foreclosure and become current on the mortgage again.

REO: See "real-estate owned."

Servicer: The lender (usually a bank) that the borrower entered into a mortgage contract with. The lender often sells the actual loan to an investor, but still serves as the administrator of the loan.

Short sale: A property sale that takes place, with the lender's permission, where the net proceeds of that sale will be less than the balance owing on the mortgage to the lender. It gets its name because the home is being sold at a price that is "short" of the amount needed to pay off the mortgage.

Short sale negotiator: A third-party negotiator who uses their experience to assist a homeowner through the short sale process by assembling, checking and submitting required documentation to the lender(s) and by handling communications and negotiations between the main parties involved in a short sale.

Short sale package: The complete package of documents that is submitted to a lender when requesting that they approve a short sale. Each lender may have a slightly different list of the exact documents they require to complete a short sale package.

Subprime mortgage: A mortgage loan to a borrower who does not meet the usual lending criteria.

Underwater mortgage: A mortgage where the balance owing on the loan is greater than the current value of the home. May also be defined as a mortgage where the balance owing on the loan plus closing costs to the sale is greater than the current value of the home. See also "negative equity."

Appendix B:

Non-Recourse States And One-Action States

It is difficult to classify states simply as "recourse" or "non-recourse," because the laws are so different between them. Most states do allow for a deficiency judgment under certain conditions.

The following states are non-recourse states for most residential mortgages:

Alaska, Arizona California,, Hawaii, Minnesota, Montana, Nevada (for most residential mortgages initiated from October 2009 onward) North Carolina, North Dakota, Oklahoma, Oregon, Washington

Other states may be non-recourse (they may not try to collect on the deficiency) for certain types of debts.

One-action states are:

California, Idaho, Montana, Nevada, New York, Utah

Appendix C:

Non-Judicial States

Non-judicial states: Alabama, Alaska, Arizona, Arkansas, California, Colorado, District of Columbia, Georgia, Hawaii, Idaho, Iowa, Massachusetts, Michigan, Minnesota, Mississippi, Missouri, Montana, Nevada, New Hampshire, North Carolina, Oklahoma, Oregon, Rhode Island, South Dakota, Tennessee, Texas, Virginia, Washington, West Virginia, Wisconsin, Wyoming

The remainder of states are judicial states. Lenders also have the right to foreclose judicially in a non-judicial state if they choose.

Appendix D:

Acknowledgments

Thanks go to the following individuals for their support of this work.

Jim Brown, Windermere SCA, Inc.

Kerri H. Donovan, Alchemy Real Estate Group

Michael A. Kairys, Genesis Real Estate Company

Richard Shute, Coldwell Banker

CPSIA information can be obtained
at www.ICGtesting.com
Printed in the USA
FSHW021054061118
53584FS